Learning D3.js 4 Mappıng

Second Edition

Build cutting-edge maps and visualizations with JavaScript

Thomas Newton
Oscar Villarreal
Lars Verspohl

BIRMINGHAM - MUMBAI

Learning D3.js 4 Mapping

Second Edition

First published: December 2014

Second edition: November 2017

Production reference: 1281117

Published by Packt Publishing Ltd.
Livery Place
35 Livery Street
Birmingham
B3 2PB, UK.
ISBN: 978-1-78728-017-5

www.packtpub.com

Credits

Authors
Thomas Newton
Oscar Villarreal
Lars Verspohl

Reviewers
Andrew Reid
Xun (Brian) Wu

Commissioning Editor
Ashwin Nair

Acquisition Editor
Nitin Dasan

Content Development Editor
Sreeja Nair

Technical Editor
Leena Patil

Copy Editor
Safis Editing

Project Coordinator
Sheejal Shah

Proofreader
Safis Editing

Indexer
Rekha Nair

Graphics
Jason Monteiro

Production Coordinator
Arvindkumar Gupta

About the Authors

Thomas Newton has over 20 years of experience in software engineering, creating highly scalable and flexible software solutions for clients. During this period, he has developed a broad range of expertise ranging from data visualizations, to large-scale cloud platforms, to continuous delivery and DevOps. When not going in a new technology, he spends time with his beautiful family.

Many thanks to Silvi, Garrett, Alex, and Cate for your endless support and love. A very special thank you to Gwen Newton for extra support and proofreading.

Oscar Villarreal has been building web applications and visualizations for the past 15 years. He's worked with all kinds of businesses and organizations globally, helping them visualize and interact with data in more meaningful ways. He enjoys spending time with his wife and kid, as well as hanging from the edge of a rock wall when climbing.

Many thanks to Caitlin and Mateo, for always being there and patiently waiting for my weekly returns.

Lars Verspohl has been modeling and visualizing data for over 15 years. He works with businesses and organisations from all over the world to turn their often complex data into intelligible interactive visualizations. He also writes and builds stuff at datamake.io. His ideal weekend is spent either at a lake or on a mountain with his kids, although it can be hard to tear them away from the computer games he wrote for them.

Many thanks to Sebastian Gutierrez for making this happen and Olly Otley for tireless proofreading.

About the Reviewers

Andrew Reid is a GIS specialist, despite an initial academic focus in the humanities, living and working in the Yukon Territory, Canada. Andrew has been exploring the world of D3 for several years, especially in relation to its geographic capacities. While he spends a disproportionate amount of time programming and working with geographic data in the long northern winter, Andrew makes full use of the summer's midnight sun, exploring and enjoying the northern wilderness.

Xun (Brian) Wu has more than 15 years of experience in web/mobile development, big data analytics, cloud computing, blockchain, and IT architecture.
Xun holds a master's degree in computer science from NJIT. He is always enthusiastic about exploring new ideas, technologies, and opportunities that arise. He always keeps himself up to date by coding, reading books, and researching.
He has previously reviewed more than 40 Packt Publishing books.

I would like to thank my family and beautiful daughters Bridget and Charlotte for their patience and support throughout this endeavor.

www.PacktPub.com

For support files and downloads related to your book, please visit www.PacktPub.com.

Did you know that Packt offers eBook versions of every book published, with PDF and ePub files available? You can upgrade to the eBook version at www.PacktPub.com and as a print book customer, you are entitled to a discount on the eBook copy. Get in touch with us at service@packtpub.com for more details.

At www.PacktPub.com, you can also read a collection of free technical articles, sign up for a range of free newsletters and receive exclusive discounts and offers on Packt books and eBooks.

https://www.packtpub.com/mapt

Get the most in-demand software skills with Mapt. Mapt gives you full access to all Packt books and video courses, as well as industry-leading tools to help you plan your personal development and advance your career.

Why subscribe?

- Fully searchable across every book published by Packt
- Copy and paste, print, and bookmark content
- On demand and accessible via a web browser

Customer Feedback

Thanks for purchasing this Packt book. At Packt, quality is at the heart of our editorial process. To help us improve, please leave us an honest review on this book's Amazon page at https://www.amazon.com/dp/1787280179.

If you'd like to join our team of regular reviewers, you can e-mail us at customerreviews@packtpub.com. We award our regular reviewers with free eBooks and videos in exchange for their valuable feedback. Help us be relentless in improving our products!

Table of Contents

Preface

This book explores the JavaScript library D3. js and its ability to help us create maps and amazing visualizations. You will no longer be confined to third-party tools in order to get a nice looking map. With D3. js, you can build your own maps and customize them as you please. This book will go from the basics of SVG, Canvas, and JavaScript, through to data trimming and modification with TopoJSON. Using D3. js to glue together these key ingredients, we will create very attractive maps that cover many common use cases, such as choropleths, data overlays on maps, interactivity, and performance.

What this book covers

Chapter 1, *Gathering Your Cartography Toolbox*, starts off with a working example in order to get a feel for what you will be able to build by the end of the book.

Chapter 2, *Creating Images from Simple Text*, dives into SVG and its common geographic shapes and attributes. Showcases how one can animate with vectors.

Chapter 3, *Producing Graphics from Data - the Foundations of D3*, reads about the foundations of the different states within D3 and how it interacts with the DOM.

Chapter 4, *Creating a Map*, presents our first examples of building maps. The chapter covers basic events and extending past map borders, as we intertwine the map with other data sets.

Chapter 5, *Click-Click Boom! Applying Interactivity to Your Map*, dives into all the types of interactions you can have with a map in your browser. This includes hovering, panning, zooming, and so on.

Chapter 6, *Finding and Working with Geographic Data*, shows how to find and utilize geospatial data.

Chapter 7, *Testing*, describes how to structure your codebase in order to have reusable chart components that are easily unit tested and primed for reuse in future projects.

Chapter 8, *Drawing with Canvas and D3*, shows how to get started with Canvas. You'll learn to draw, animate, and use the D3 life cycle for data updates.

Chapter 9, *Mapping with Canvas and D3*, describes how to map and animate thousands of points with Canvas, as well as how Canvas animation compares to SVG animation.

Chapter 10, *Adding Interactivity to Your Canvas Map*, guides you through the process of adding interactivity to Canvas, a process that requires a little more thought and attention than with SVG.

Chapter 11, *Shaping Maps with Data – Hexbin Maps*, explains how to build hexbin maps with D3 - a great way to show geospatial point data.

Chapter 12, *Publishing a Visualization with GitHub Pages*, shows you how to get your visualization online in a simple and fast way.

What you need for this book

The following are the requirements for this book; these work on macOS, Windows, and Linux:

- A D3.js library v4.12.0
- Node.js v8.9.0+
- npm for example, v5.5.1+

Who this book is for

This book is for people with at least a basic knowledge of web development (basic HTML/CSS/JavaScript). You don't need to have worked with D3.js before.

Conventions

In this book, you will find a number of text styles that distinguish between different kinds of information. Here are some examples of these styles and an explanation of their meaning.

Code words in text, database table names, folder names, filenames, file extensions, pathnames, dummy URLs, user input, and Twitter handles are shown as follows: "The width and height are the only properties the canvas element has."

A block of code is set as follows:

```
context.save();
context.translate(140, 190);
context.fillRect(0, 0, 60, 30);
context.restore();
```

New terms and **important words** are shown in bold. Words that you see on the screen, for example, in menus or dialog boxes, appear in the text like this: "You go to `https://github. com/`, click on **Sign in**, and follow the steps."

Warnings or important notes appear in a box like this.

Tips and tricks appear like this.

Reader feedback

Feedback from our readers is always welcome. Let us know what you think about this book-what you liked or disliked. Reader feedback is important for us as it helps us develop titles that you will really get the most out of.

To send us general feedback, simply e-mail `feedback@packtpub.com`, and mention the book's title in the subject of your message.

If there is a topic that you have expertise in and you are interested in either writing or contributing to a book, see our author guide at `www.packtpub.com/authors`.

Customer support

Now that you are the proud owner of a Packt book, we have a number of things to help you to get the most from your purchase.

Downloading the example code

You can download the example code files for this book from your account at `http://www. packtpub.com`. If you purchased this book elsewhere, you can visit `http://www.packtpub. com/support` and register to have the files e-mailed directly to you.

You can download the code files by following these steps:

1. Log in or register to our website using your e-mail address and password.
2. Hover the mouse pointer on the **SUPPORT** tab at the top.
3. Click on **Code Downloads & Errata**.
4. Enter the name of the book in the **Search** box.
5. Select the book for which you're looking to download the code files.
6. Choose from the drop-down menu where you purchased this book from.
7. Click on **Code Download**.

You can also download the code files by clicking on the **Code Files** button on the book's webpage at the Packt Publishing website. This page can be accessed by entering the book's name in the **Search** box. Please note that you need to be logged in to your Packt account.

Once the file is downloaded, please make sure that you unzip or extract the folder using the latest version of:

- WinRAR / 7-Zip for Windows
- Zipeg / iZip / UnRarX for Mac
- 7-Zip / PeaZip for Linux

The code bundle for the book is also hosted on GitHub at https://github.com/ PacktPublishing/Learning-D3js-4-Mapping-Second-Edition. We also have other code bundles from our rich catalog of books and videos available at https://github.com/ PacktPublishing/. Check them out!

Downloading the color images of this book

We also provide you with a PDF file that has color images of the screenshots/diagrams used in this book. The color images will help you better understand the changes in the output. You can download this file from https://www.packtpub.com/sites/default/files/ downloads/LearningD3dotjs4MappingSecondEdition_ColorImages.pdf.

Errata

Although we have taken every care to ensure the accuracy of our content, mistakes do happen. If you find a mistake in one of our books-maybe a mistake in the text or the code- we would be grateful if you could report this to us. By doing so, you can save other readers from frustration and help us improve subsequent versions of this book. If you find any errata, please report them by visiting http://www.packtpub.com/submit-errata, selecting your book, clicking on the **Errata Submission Form** link, and entering the details of your errata. Once your errata are verified, your submission will be accepted and the errata will be uploaded to our website or added to any list of existing errata under the Errata section of that title.

To view the previously submitted errata, go to https://www.packtpub.com/books/content/support and enter the name of the book in the search field. The required information will appear under the **Errata** section.

Piracy

Piracy of copyrighted material on the Internet is an ongoing problem across all media. At Packt, we take the protection of our copyright and licenses very seriously. If you come across any illegal copies of our works in any form on the Internet, please provide us with the location address or website name immediately so that we can pursue a remedy.

Please contact us at copyright@packtpub.com with a link to the suspected pirated material.

We appreciate your help in protecting our authors and our ability to bring you valuable content.

Questions

If you have a problem with any aspect of this book, you can contact us at questions@packtpub.com, and we will do our best to address the problem.

1

Gathering Your Cartography Toolbox

Welcome to the world of cartography with D3. In this chapter, you will be given all the tools you need to create a map using D3. These tools exist freely and openly, thanks to the wonderful world of open source. Given that we are going to be speaking in terms of the web, our languages will be HTML, CSS, and JavaScript. After reading this book, you will be able to use all three languages effectively in order to create maps on your own.

In this chapter, we will cover the following topics:

- Quick bootstrap
- Step-by-step bootstrap
- Installing key libraries and tools
- Using the web browser as a development tool

When creating maps in D3, your toolbox is extraordinarily light. The goal is to focus on creating data visualizations and remove the burden of heavy IDEs and map-making software.

Quick bootstrap

The following instructions assume that Node.js , npm, and git are already installed on your system. If not, feel free to follow the *Step-by-Step bootstrap* section.

Type the following in the command line to install a light webserver::

```
npm install -g http-server
```

Install TopoJSON:

```
npm install -g topojson
```

Clone the sample code with included libraries:

```
git clone --depth=1 git@github.com:climboid/d3jsMaps.git
```

Go to the root project:

```
cd d3jsMaps
```

To start the server type the following:

```
http-server
```

> You can download the example code files from your account at http://www.packtpub.com for all the Packt Publishing books you have purchased. If you purchased this book elsewhere, you can visit http://www.packtpub.com/support and register to have the files emailed directly to you.

Now, open your web browser to http://localhost:8080/chapter-1/example-1.html, and you should see the following map:

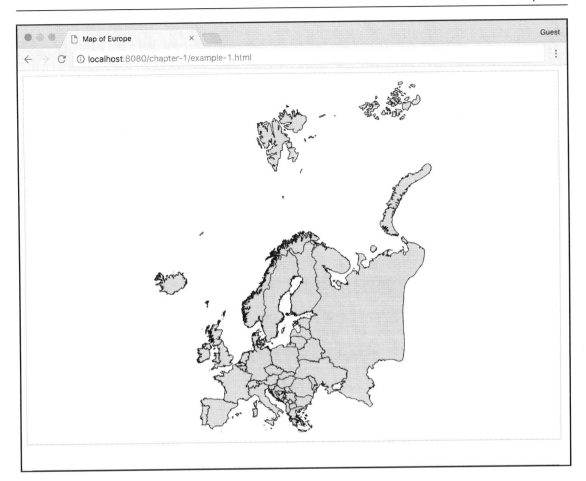

Step-by-step bootstrap

The next section covers detailed instructions to set up your development environment if you do not have any of the required packages. By the end of the chapter, you will have a working environment for the rest of the book (an example of a running map and an initial look at tools used to create visualizations).

A lightweight web server

Technically, most of the content we will craft can render directly in the browser without the use of a web server. However, we highly recommend you do not go ahead with this approach. Running a web server in your local development environment is extremely easy and provides several benefits:

- Geographic information, statistical data, and visualization code can be clearly separated into isolated files
- API calls can be stubbed and simulated, allowing easy integration into a full-stack application in the future
- It will prevent common mistakes when making AJAX calls to fetch geographic and statistical data (for example, the same-origin policy)

For our choice of web server and other tools in our toolbox, we will rely on a Node.js package named `http-server`. Node.js is a platform built on Chrome's JavaScript runtime, which is used to build fast, scalable network applications. The platform includes **Node Package Manager (npm)**, which was created by other members of the vibrant Node.js community and allows the developer to quickly install packages of pre-built software.

To install Node.js, simply perform the following steps:

1. Go to the website `http://nodejs.org`.
2. Click on the **INSTALL** button.
3. Open the downloaded package and follow the defaults.

To test the installation, type the following in the command line:

```
node -v
```

Something similar should return:

```
v0.10.26
```

This means we have installed the given version of Node.js.

TopoJSON is a command-line utility used to create files in the TopoJSON-serialized format. The TopoJSON format will be discussed in detail in `Chapter 6`, *Finding and Working with Geographic Data*. The TopoJSON utility is also installed via `npm`.

We have already installed Node.js and npm, so enter the following on the command line:

```
npm install -g topojson
```

Once the installation is complete, you should check the version of TopoJSON installed on your machine just as we did with Node.js:

```
geo2topo --version
```

If you see version 3.x, it means you have successfully installed TopoJSON.

> TopoJSON uses node-gyp which has several dependencies based on the operating system. Please go to http://github.com/TooTallNate/node-gyp for details.

If you're using Windows, the basic steps to get TopoJSON working are as follows:

1. Install Python 2.x (3.x not supported at the time of writing this book).
2. Install Microsoft Visual Studio C++ 2012 for Desktop (Express).

Using the web browser as a development tool

Although any modern browser supports **Scalable Vector Graphics (SVG)** and has some kind of console, we strongly recommend you use Google Chrome for these examples. It comes bundled with developer tools that will allow you to very easily open, explore, and modify the code. If you are not using Google Chrome, please go to http://www.google.com/chrome and install Google Chrome.

Installing the sample code

Go to https://github.com/climboid/d3jsMaps and either clone the repo, if you are familiar with Git cloning, or simply download the zipped version. Once it is downloaded, make sure to extract the file if you have it zipped.

Use the command prompt or terminal to go to the directory where you downloaded your file. For instance, if you downloaded the file to your desktop, type in the following:

```
cd ~/Desktop/d3jsMaps
```

To start the server type the following:

```
http-server
```

The last command will launch the simple server we installed previously for the supplied sample code. This means that, if you open your browser and go to `http://localhost:8080/chapter-1/example-1.html,` you should see a map of Europe, similar to the one shown earlier.

Working with the developer tools

It's time to open the developer tools. In the top-right corner of the browser, you will see the icon as shown in the following screenshot:

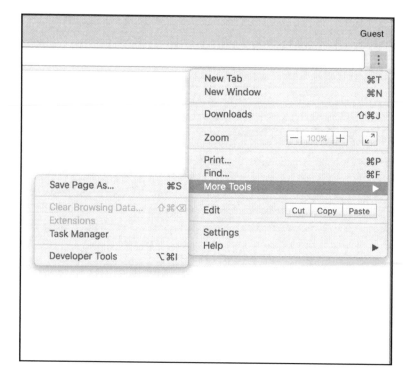

This icon opens a submenu. Click on **More Tools**, then click on **Developer tools**.
A panel will open at the bottom of the browser, containing all the developer tools at your disposal.

> The option names mentioned here might differ according to the version of Chrome you are using.

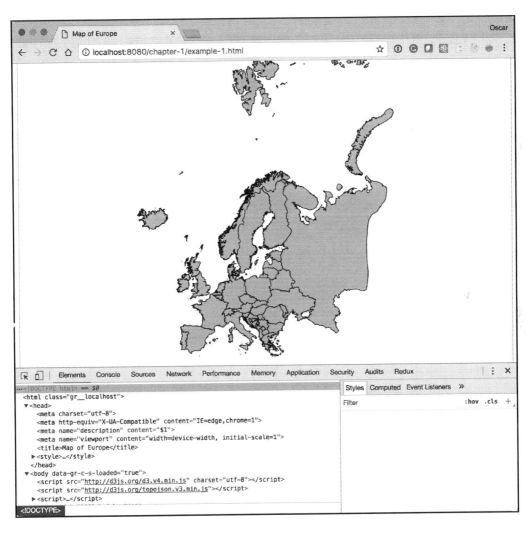

For quick access to developer tools on the Mac, use *alt* + command + *I*; for Windows PCs, use *Ctrl + Shift + I*.

Within developer tools, you have a series of tabs (**Elements, Network, Sources,** and so on). These tools are extremely valuable and will allow you to inspect different aspects of your code. For more information on the Chrome developer tools, please go to this link: `https://developer.chrome.com/devtools/docs/authoring-development-workflow`.

Since we are going to focus on the **Elements** tab, click on it if it is not already selected.

You should see something similar to the preceding screenshot; it will have the following code statement:

```
<svg width="812" height="584">
```

If you click on the SVG item, you should see it expand and display the path tag. The path tag will have several numbers and characters tied to a d attribute. These numbers are control points that draw the path. We will cover how the path is drawn in the next chapter and how path tags are used to create maps in Chapter 4, *Creating a Map* and Chapter 5, *Click-Click Boom! Applying Interactivity to Your Map*.

We also want to draw your attention to how the HTML5 application loads the D3 library. Again, in the **Elements** tag, after the SVG tag, you should see the `<script>` tag pointing to D3.js and TopoJSON:

```
<script src="http://d3js.org/d3.v4.min.js"></script>
<script src="http://d3js.org/topojson.v3.min.js"></script>
```

If you click on the path located inside the SVG tag, you will see a new panel called the CSS inspector or the styles inspector. It shows and controls all the styles that are applied to a selected element, in this case, the path element.

These three components create a D3 visualization:

- HTML5 (the SVG and path elements)
- JavaScript (the D3.js library and map code)
- CSS (the styling of the HTML5 elements)

Creating maps and visualizations using these three components will be discussed and analyzed throughout the book.

Summary

This chapter reveals a quick glimpse of the steps for basic setup in order to have a well-organized codebase to create maps with D3. You should become familiar with this setup because we will be using this convention throughout the book.

The remaining chapters will focus on creating detailed maps and achieving realistic visualizations through HTML, JavaScript, and CSS.

Let's go!

2
Creating Images from Simple Text

In this chapter, a high-level overview of **Scalable Vector Graphics (SVG)** will be presented by explaining how it operates and what elements it encompasses. In a browser context, SVG is very similar to HTML and is one of the means by which D3 expresses its power. Understanding the nodes and attributes of SVG will empower us to create many kinds of visualizations, not just maps. This chapter includes the following points:

- A general overview of SVG and its key elements
- The SVG coordinate system
- The primary elements of SVG (lines, rectangles, circles, polygons, and paths)

SVG, an XML markup language, is designed to describe two-dimensional vector graphics. The SVG markup language resides in the DOM as a node that describes exactly how to draw a shape (a curve, line, circle, or polygon). Just like HTML, SVG tags can also be styled from standard CSS. Note that, because all commands reside in the DOM, the more shapes you have, the more nodes you have and the more work for the browser. This is important to remember because, as SVG visualizations become more complex, the less fluidly they will perform.

The main SVG node is declared as follows:

```
<svg width="200" height="200"></svg>
```

This node's basic properties are width and height; they provide the primary container for the other nodes that make up a visualization. For example, if you wanted to create 10 sequential circles in a 200×200 box, the tags would look like this:

```
<?xml version="1.0"?>
<svg width="200" height="200">
  <circle cx="60" cy="60" r="50"/>
  <circle cx ="5" cy="5" r="10"/>
  <circle cx="25" cy="35" r="45"/>
  <circle cx="180" cy="180" r="10"/>
  <circle cx="80" cy="130" r="40"/>
  <circle cx="50" cy="50" r="5"/>
  <circle cx="2" cy="2" r="7"/>
  <circle cx="77" cy="77" r="17"/>
  <circle cx="100" cy="100" r="40"/>
  <circle cx="146" cy="109" r="22"/>
</svg>
```

Note that 10 circles would need 10 nodes in the DOM, plus its container.

SVG contains several primitives that allow the developer to draw shapes quickly. We will cover the following primitives throughout this chapter:

- circle: A standard circle with a defined radius and position attributes
- rect: A standard rectangle with height, width, and position attributes
- polygon: Any polygon, described by a list of points
- line: A line with start and end points
- path: A complex line created through a series of drawing commands

The SVG coordinate system

What about position? Where do these primitives draw inside the SVG element? What if you wanted to put a circle in the top-left and another one bottom-right? Where do you start?

SVG is positioned by a grid system, similar to the Cartesian coordinate system. However, in SVG (0,0) is the top-left corner. The x axis proceeds horizontally from left to right starting at 0. The y axis also starts at 0 and extends downward. See the following illustration:

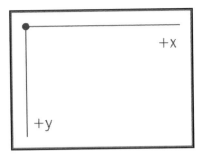

What about drawing shapes on top of each other? How do you control the *z* index? In SVG, there is no *z* coordinate. Depth is determined by the order in which the shape is drawn. If you were to draw a circle with coordinates (10,10) and then another one with coordinates (10,10), you would see the second circle drawn on top of the first.

The following sections will cover the basic SVG primitives for drawing shapes and some of their most common attributes.

Line

The SVG line is one of the simplest in the library. It draws a straight line from one point to another. The syntax is very straightforward and can be experimented with at: `http://localhost:8080/chapter-2/line.html`, assuming the HTTP server is running:

```
<line x1="10" y1="10" x2="100" y2="100" stroke-width="1"
 stroke="red"/>
```

This will give you the following output:

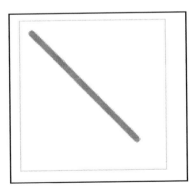

A description of the element's attributes is as follows:

- x1 and y1: The starting x and y coordinates
- x2 and y2: The ending x and y coordinates
- stroke: This gives the line a red color
- stroke-width: This denotes the width of the line to be drawn in pixels

The line tag also has the ability to change the style of the end of the line. For example, adding the following would change the image so it has round ends:

```
stroke-linecap: round;
```

As stated earlier, all SVG tags can also be styled with CSS elements. An alternative way of producing the same graphic would be to first create a CSS style, as shown in the following code:

```
line {
    stroke: red;
    stroke-linecap: round;
    stroke-width: 5;
}
```

Then you can create a very simple SVG tag using the following code:

```
<line x1="10" y1="10" x2="100" y2="100"></line>
```

More complex lines, as well as curves, can be achieved with the path tag; we will cover it in the *Path* section.

Rectangle

The basic HTML code to create a rectangle is as follows:

```
<rect width="100" height="20" x="10" y="10"></rect>
```

Let's apply the following style:

```
rect {
    stroke-width: 1;
    stroke:steelblue;
    fill:#888;
    fill-opacity: .5;
}
```

We will create a rectangle that starts at the coordinates (10,10), and is 100 pixels wide and 20 pixels high. Based on the styling, it will have a blue outline, a gray interior, and will appear slightly opaque. See the following output and example `http://localhost:8080/chapter-2/rectangle.html`:

There are two more attributes that are useful when creating rounded borders (rx and ry):

```
<rect with="100" height="20" x="10" y="10" rx="5" ry="5"></rect>
```

These attributes indicate that the x and y corners will have 5-pixel curves.

Circle

A circle is positioned with the cx and cy attributes. These indicate the *x* and *y* coordinates of the center of the circle. The radius is determined by the r attribute. The following is an example you can experiment with (`http://localhost:8080/chapter-2/circle.html`):

```
<circle cx="62" cy="62" r="50"></circle>
```

Now type in the following code:

```
circle {
     stroke-width: 5;
     stroke:steelblue;
     fill:#888;
     fill-opacity: .5;
}
```

This will create a circle with the familiar blue outline, a gray interior, and half-way opaque.

Polygon

To create a polygon, use the `polygon` tag. The best way to think about an SVG polygon is to compare it to a child's dot-to-dot game. You can imagine a series of dots and a pen connecting each (*x*, *y*) coordinate with a straight line. The series of *dots* is identified in the `points` attribute. Take the following as an example (`http://localhost:8080/chapter-2/polygon.html`):

```
<polygon points="60,5 10,120 115,120"/>
```

First, we start at `60,5` and we move to `10,120`. Then, we proceed to `115,120` and, finally, return to `60,5`.

The pen returns to the starting position automatically.

Path

When creating maps with D3, the `path` SVG tag is used most often. Using the definition from W3C, you can think of the `path` tag as a series of commands that explain how to draw any shape by moving a pen on a piece of paper. The `path` commands start with the location to place the pen and then a series of follow-up commands that tell the pen how to connect additional points with lines. The `path` shapes can also be filled or have their outline styled.

Let's look at a very simple example to replicate the triangle we created as a polygon.

Open your browser, go to `http://localhost:8080/chapter-2/path.html`, and you will see the following output on your screen:

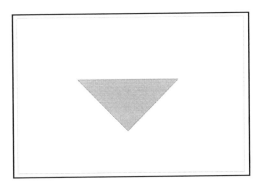

Right-click anywhere in the triangle and select **Inspect element**.

The `path` command for this shape is as follows:

```
<path d="M 120 120 L 220 220, 420 120 Z" stroke="steelblue"
    fill="lightyellow" stroke-width="2"></path>
```

The attribute that contains the path-drawing commands is `d`. The commands adhere to the following structure:

- `M`: Put the pen down to start drawing at `x = 120 y = 120`
- `L`: Draw a straight line that connects (120,120) to `x = 220 y = 220`, then draw another straight line that connects (220,220) to `x = 420 y = 120`
- `Z`: Connect the last data point (420,120) to where we started (120,120)

Experiment

Let's try some experiments to reinforce what we just learned. From the Chrome developer tools, simply remove the z at the end of the path, and hit *Enter*:

```
▼<svg height="300" width="450">
    <path d="M 120 120 L 220 220, 320 120 Z"></path>
  </svg>
```

You should see the top line disappear. Try some other experiments with changing the data points in the L subcommand.

Paths with curves

Paths can also have curves. The concept is still the same; you connect several data points with lines. The main difference is that now you apply a curve to each line as it connects the dots. There are three types of curve commands:

- Cubic Bézier
- Quadratic Bézier
- Elliptical arc

Each command is explained in detail at http://www.w3.org/TR/SVG11/paths.html. As an example, let's apply a cubic Bézier curve to the triangle. The format for the command is as follows:

```
C x1 y1 x2 y2 x y
```

This command can be inserted into the path structure at any point:

- C: Indicates that we are applying a Cubic Bézier curve, just as L in the previous example indicates a straight line
- x1 and y1: Adds a control point to influence the curve's tangent
- x2 and y2: Adds a second control point after applying x1 and y1
- x and y: Indicates the final resting place of the line

To apply this command to our previous triangle, we need to replace the second line command (`320 120`) with a cubic command (`C 200 70 480 290 320 120`).

Before, the statement was as follows:

```
<path d="M 120 120 L 220 220, 320 120 Z"></path>
```

After adding the cubic command, it will be as follows:

```
<path d="M 120 120 L 220 220, C 200 70 480 290 320 120 Z"></path>
```

This will produce the following shape:

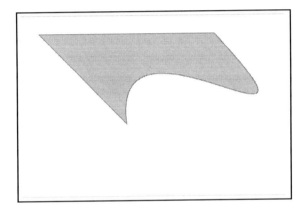

To illustrate how the cubic Bézier curve works, let's draw circles and lines to show the control points in the `C` command:

```
<svg  height="300" width="525">
    <path d="M 120 120 L 220 220 C 200 70 480 290 320 120 Z ">
    </path>
    <line x1="220"  y1="220" x2="200" y2="70"></line>
    <circle cx="200" cy="70" r="5" ></circle>
    <line x1="200"  y1="70"  x2="480" y2="290"></line>
    <circle cx="480" cy="290"  r="5"></circle>
    <line x1="480"  y1="290" x2="320" y2="120"></line>
</svg>
```

The output should look like the one shown in the following screenshot, and can be experimented with at http://localhost:8080/chapter-2/curves.html. You can see the angles created by the control points (indicated by circles in the output) and the cubic Bézier curves applied.

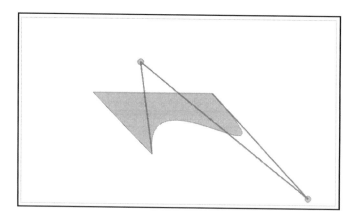

SVG paths are the main tool leveraged when drawing geographic regions. However, imagine if you were to draw an entire map by hand using SVG paths; the task would become exhausting! For example, the command structure for the map of Europe in our first chapter has 3,366,121 characters in it! Even a simple state such as Colorado would be a lot of code if executed by hand:

```
<path xmlns="http://www.w3.org/2000/svg" id="CO_1_"
style="fill:#ff0000" d="M 115.25800,104.81000 L
116.51200,84.744000 L 117.00000,77.915000 L 106.82700,77.077000 L
99.371000,76.452000 L 88.014000,75.198000 L 81.709000,74.431000 L
80.907000,81.189000 L 79.932000,88.018000 L 78.788000,96.547000 L
78.329000,99.932000 L 78.154000,101.11800 L 88.641000,102.37200 L
99.898000,103.72200 L 109.88400,104.39200 L 111.91300,104.60300 L
115.39700,104.77700"/>
```

We will learn in later chapters how D3 will come to the rescue.

Transform

The `transform` allows you to change your visualization dynamically and is one of the advantages of using SVG and commands to draw shapes. Transform is an additional attribute you can add to any of the elements we have discussed so far. Two important types of `transform` when dealing with our D3 maps are:

- **Translate**: Move the element
- **Scale**: Adjust the coordinates for all attributes in the element

Translate

You will likely use this transformation in all of your cartography work and will see it in most D3 examples online. As a technique, it's often used with a margin object to shift the entire visualization. The following syntax can be applied to any element:

```
transform="translate(x,y)"
```

Here, x and y are the coordinates to move the element by.

For example, a translate `transform` can move our circle 50 pixels to the left and 50 pixels down by using the following code:

```
<circle cx="62" cy="62" r="50" transform="translate(50,50)"></circle>
```

Here is the output:

Note that the translucent image represents the original image and the location the shape moved from. The `translate` attribute is not an absolute position. It adjusts the origin of the circle relatively to cx, cy and adds 50 to those coordinates. If you were to move the circle to the top-left of the container, you would translate with negative values. For example:

```
transform="translate(-10,-10)"
```

Feel free to experiment with your Chrome developer tools or code editor at `http://localhost:8080/chapter-2/translate.html`.

Scale

The scale transform is easy to understand but often creates undesired effects if you lose the focus of where the scaling originated.

Scale adjusts the (*x*, *y*) values across all attributes in the element. Using the earlier `circle` code, we have the following:

```
<circle cx="62" cy="62" r="50" stroke-width="5" fill="red"
    transform="scale(2,2)"></circle>
```

The scale is going to double the cx, cy, radius, and `stroke-width`, producing the following output (`http://localhost:8080/chapter-2/scale.html`):

It is important to emphasize that, because we are using SVG commands to draw the shapes, there is no loss of quality as we scale the images, unlike raster images such as PNG or JPEG. The transform types can be combined to adjust for scale, altering the *x* and *y* position of the shape. Let's use the `path` example that we used earlier in the following code:

```
<path d="M 120 120 L 220 220 C 200 70 480 290 320 120 Z"
   stroke="steelblue" fill="lightyellow" stroke-width="2"
   transform="translate(-200,-200), scale(2,2)"></path>
```

The preceding code will produce the following output
(`http://localhost:8080/chapter-2/scale_translate.html`):

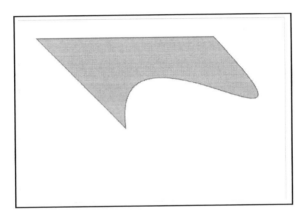

Grouping

The group tag `<g>` is used often in SVG, especially in maps. It is used to group elements and then apply a set of attributes to that set. It provides the following benefits:

- It allows you to treat a set of shapes as a single shape for the purpose of scaling and translating.
- It prevents code duplication by allowing you to set attributes at a higher level and have them inherit all the elements included.
- Groups are essential for applying transformations to large sets of SVG nodes in a performant manner. Grouping offsets the parent group rather than modifying each of the attributes in every item of the group.

Let's take the set of shapes used to explain Bézier curves and add all of them to a single group, combining everything we have learned so far, in the following code:

```
<svg height="500" width="800">
  <g transform="translate(-200,-100), scale(2,2)">
    <path d="M 120 120 L 220 220 C 200 70 480 290 320 120 Z">
    </path>

    <line x1="220" y1="220" x2="200" y2="70"></line>
    <circle cx="200" cy="70" r="5" ></circle>

    <line x1="200" y1="70" x2="480" y2="290"></line>
    <circle cx="480" cy="290" r="5" ></circle>

    <line x1="480" y1="290" x2="320" y2="120"></line>
  </g>
</svg>
```

The preceding code will produce the following image
(`http://localhost:8080/chapter-2/group.html`):

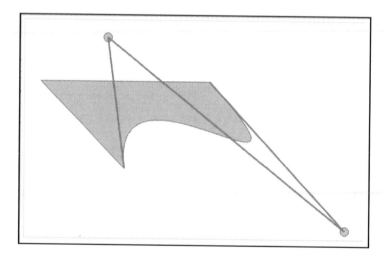

Without using the group element, we would have had to apply a transform, translate, and scale to all six shapes in the set. Grouping helps us save time and allows us to make quick alignment tweaks in the future.

Text

The text element, as its name describes, is used to display text in SVG. The basic HTML code to create a text node is as follows:

```
<text x="250" y="150">Hello world!</text>
```

It has an x and a y coordinate to tell it where to begin writing in the SVG coordinate system. Styling can be achieved with a CSS class in order to have a clear separation of concerns within our code base. For example, check out the following code:

```
<text x="250" y="150" class="myText">Hello world!</text>

.myText{
  font-size:22px;
  font-family:Helvetica;
  stroke-width:2;
}
```

Text also supports rotation in order to provide flexibility when positioning it on the visualization:

```
<svg width="600" height="600">
      <text x="250" y="150" class="myText"
      transform="rotate(45,200,0)" font-family="Verdana"
      font-size="100">Hello world!</text>
</svg>;
```

Some examples are located at `http://localhost:8080/chapter-2/text.html` and displayed as shown in the following image:

Keep in mind that, if you rotate the text, it will rotate relative to its origin (x and y). You can specify the origin of the translation via `cx` and `cy`, or in this case `250,150`. See the `transform` property in the code for more clarity.

Summary

This chapter has given us a wealth of information regarding SVG. We explained paths, lines, circles, rectangles, text, and some of their attributes. We also covered transformation by scaling and translating shapes. Since this chapter has given us a solid baseline, we can now create complicated shapes. The next chapter will introduce us to D3 and how it is used to manage SVG programmatically. On we go!

3
Producing Graphics from Data - the Foundations of D3

We have acquired our toolbox and reviewed the basics of SVG. It is now time to explore D3.js. D3 is the evolution of the Protovis (http://mbostock.github.io/protovis/) library. If you have already delved into data visualization have been interested in making charts for your web application, you might have already used this library. Additional libraries also exist that can be differentiated by how quickly they rendered graphics and their compatibility with different browsers. For example, Internet Explorer did not support SVG but used its own implementation, VML. This made the Raphaël.js library an excellent option because it automatically mapped to either VML or SVG. On the other hand, jqPlot was easy to use, and its simplistic jQuery plugin interface allowed developers to adopt it very quickly.

However, Protovis had something different. Given the vector nature of the library, it allowed you to illustrate different kinds of visualizations, as well as generate fluid transitions. Please feel free to look at the links provided and see for yourself. Examine the force-directed layout at: http://mbostock.github.io/protovis/ex/force.html. In 2010, these were interesting and compelling visualizations, especially for the browser.

Inspired by Protovis, a team at Stanford University (consisting of Jeff Heer, Mike Bostock, and Vadim Ogievetsky) began to focus on D3. D3, and its application to SVG, gave developers an easy way to bind their visualizations to data and add interactivity.

There is a wealth of information available for researching D3. A great resource for complete coverage can be found on the D3 website at: `https://github.com/mbostock/d3/wiki`. In this chapter, we will introduce the following concepts that will be used throughout this book:

- Creating basic SVG elements
- The `enter()` function
- The `update` function
- The `exit()` function
- AJAX

Creating basic SVG elements

A common operation in D3 is to select a DOM element and append SVG elements. Subsequent calls will then set the SVG attributes, which we learned about in Chapter 2, *Creating Images from Simple Text*. D3 accomplishes this operation through an easy-to-read, functional syntax called **method chaining**. Let's walk through a very simple example to illustrate how this is accomplished (go to `http://localhost:8080/chapter-3/example-1.html` if you have the http-server running):

```
var svg = d3.select("body")
    .append("svg")
    .attr("width", 200)
    .attr("height", 200)
```

First, we select the `body` tag and append an SVG element to it. This SVG element has a width and height of 200 pixels. We also store the selection in a variable:

```
svg.append('rect')
    .attr('x', 10)
    .attr('y', 10)
    .attr("width",50)
    .attr("height",100);
```

Next, we use the `svg` variable and append a `<rect>` item to it. This `rect` item will start at (10,10) and will have a width of 50 and a height of 100. From your Chrome browser, open the Chrome developer tools with the **Elements** tab selected and inspect the SVG element:

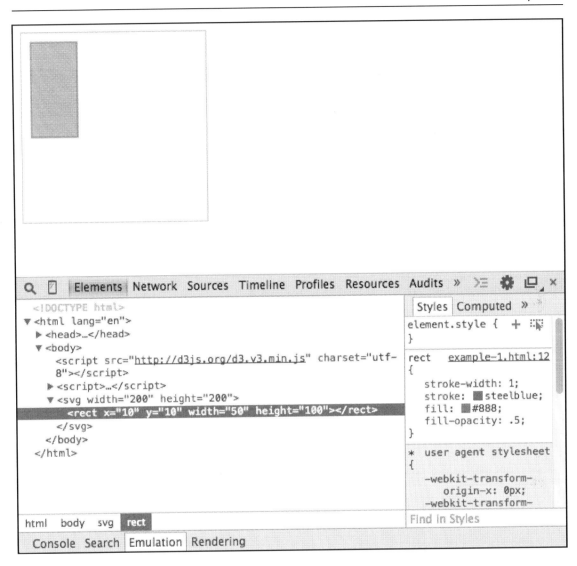

Notice the pattern: `append('svg')` creates `<svg></svg>`. `attr('width',200)` and `attr('height',200)` sets `width="200"` and `height="200"` respectively. Together, they produce the SVG syntax we learned about in the previous chapter:

```
<svg width="200" height="200">...</svg>
```

The enter() function

The `enter()` function is a part of every basic D3 visualization. It allows the developer to define a starting point with attached data. The `enter()` function can be thought of as a section of code that executes when data is applied to the visualization for the first time. Typically, the `enter()` function will follow the selection of a DOM element. Let's walk through an example (`http://localhost:8080/chapter-3/example-2.html`):

```
var svg = d3.select("body")
    .append("svg")
    .attr("width", 200)
    .attr("height", 200);
```

Create the SVG container as we did earlier, as follows:

```
svg.selectAll('rect').data([1,2]).enter()
```

The `data` function is the way we bind data to our selection. In this example, we are binding a very simple array, `[1,2]`, to the selection `<rect>`. The `enter()` function will loop through the `[1,2]` array and apply the subsequent function calls, as shown in the following code:

```
.append('rect')
.attr('x', function(d){ return d*20; })
.attr('y', function(d){ return d*50; })
```

As we loop through each element in the array, we will do the following:

- Append a new `rect` SVG element
- Position the `rect` element in coordinates $x = d * 20$ and $y = d * 50$ for the element, where d is equal to 1 for the first element and 2 for the second element, as shown in the following code:

```
.attr("width",50)
.attr("height",100);
```

We will keep `height` and `width` the same:

```
<svg width="200" height="200">
  <rect x="20" y="50" width="50" height="100"></rect>
  <rect x="40" y="100" width="50" height="100"></rect>
</svg>
```

Look closely; take a peek at the Chrome developer tools. We see two rectangles, each corresponding to one element in our array, as shown in the following screenshot:

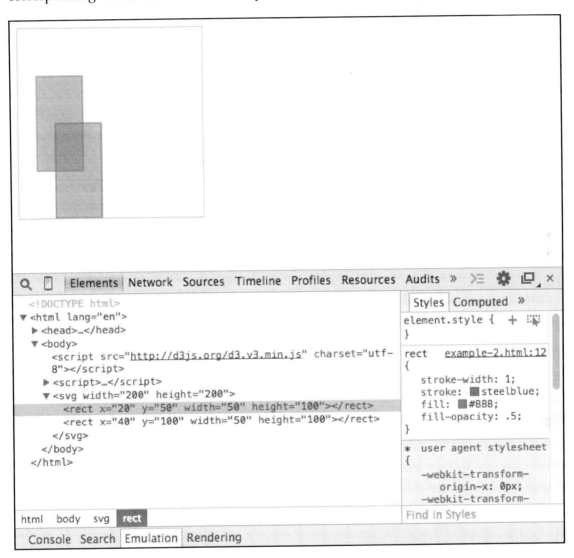

Remember, data doesn't necessarily have to be boring numbers, such as 1 or 2. The data array can consist of any data objects. To illustrate this, we will change the previous array to an array of objects in the next example
(see `http://localhost:8080/chapter-3/example-3.html`):

As you can see in the following code snippet, our data array has two objects, each one with four different key-value pairs:

```
var data = [
  {
     x:10,
     y:10,
     width:5,
     height:40
  },{
     x:40,
     y:10,
     width:100,
     height:40
  }
];

  var svg = d3.select("body")
     .append("svg")
     .attr("width", 200)
     .attr("height", 200);

  svg.selectAll('rect').data(data).enter()
     .append('rect')
     .attr('x', function(d){ return d.x})
     .attr('y', function(d){ return d.y})
     .attr("width", function(d){ return d.width})
     .attr("height", function(d){ return d.height});
```

Now, as we loop through each object in the array, we will do the following:

- Still append a new rect SVG element.
- Position and size the rect element by the properties of the object. The first rectangle will be positioned at x=10, y=10, and have a width of 5 and a height of 40. The second rectangle will be positioned at 40, 10, and will have a width of 100 and a height of 40.
- Remember that d represents the datum, or each object within the array, which is why we refer to d.x or d.y to get x and y properties accordingly.

The update function

Not only do we have our rectangles, but we've also joined them to a dataset composed of two objects. Both objects share the same properties, namely x, y, width, and height, so it's easy to loop through them and read/bind the values to our visualization. The output of this is a set of static SVG elements. This section will cover how to update the SVG elements and properties as the joined data changes. Let's enhance the previous example to explain exactly how this works (http://localhost:8080/chapter-3/example-4.html):

```
function makeData(n){
  var arr = [];

  for (var i=0; i<n; i++){
    arr.push({
      x:Math.floor((Math.random() * 100) + 1),
      y:Math.floor((Math.random() * 100) + 1),
      width:Math.floor((Math.random() * 100) + 1),
      height:Math.floor((Math.random() * 100) + 1)
    })
  };

  return arr;
}
```

This function creates a new array of objects with random properties for x, y, width, and height. We can use this to simulate a change in data, allowing us to create n number of items, all with different properties:

```
var rectangles = function(svg) {
```

Here, we create a function that inserts rectangles into the DOM on every invocation of D3. The description is as follows:

```
var data = makeData(2);
```

Let's generate our fake data:

```
var rect = svg.selectAll('rect').data(data);
```

Let's select our rectangle and assign our data to it. This gives us a variable to which we can easily apply enter() and update later. The following sections are written in a verbose way to illustrate exactly what is going on with enter(), update, and exit(). While it's possible to take shortcuts in D3, it's best to stick to the following style to prevent confusion:

```
// Enter
rect.enter().append('rect')
  .attr('test', function(d,i) {
    // Enter called 2 times only
    console.log('enter placing initial rectangle: ', i)
  });
```

As in the previous section, for each element in the array we append a rectangle tag to the DOM. If you're running this code in your Chrome browser, you will notice that the console only displays enter placing initial rectangle twice. This is because the enter() section is called only when there are more elements in the array than in the DOM:

```
// Update
rect.transition().duration(500).attr('x', function(d){
    return d.x; })
  .attr('y', function(d){ return d.y; })
  .attr('width', function(d){ return d.width; })
  .attr('height', function(d){ return d.height; })
  .attr('test', function(d, i) {
    // update every data change
    console.log('updating x position to: ', d.x)
  });
```

The `update` section is applied to every element in the original selection, excluding entered elements. In the previous example, we set the `x`, `y`, `width`, and `height` attributes of the rectangle for every data object. The `update` section is not defined with an explicit `update` method. D3 implies an `update` call if no other section is provided. If you are running the code in your Chrome browser, you will see the console display `updating x position to:` every time the data changes:

```
var svg = d3.select("body")
    .append("svg")
    .attr("width", 200)
    .attr("height", 200);
```

The following command inserts our working SVG container:

```
rectangles(svg);
```

The following command draws the first version of our visualization:

```
setInterval(function(){
    rectangles(svg);
},1000);
```

The `setInterval()` function is the JavaScript function used to execute an operation every *x* milliseconds. In this case, we are calling the `rectangles` function every `1000` milliseconds.

The `rectangles` function generates a new dataset every time it is called. It has the same property structure that we had before, but the values tied to those properties are random numbers between *1* and *100*. On the first call, the `enter()` section is invoked and we create our initial two rectangles. Every `1000` milliseconds, we reinvoke the `rectangles` function with the same data structure but different random property attributes. Because the structure is the same, the `enter()` section is now skipped and only `update` is reapplied to the existing rectangles. This is why we get the same rectangles with different dimensions every time we plot.

The `update` method is very useful. For instance, your dataset could be tied to the stock market and you could update your visualization every *n* milliseconds to reflect the changes in the stock market. You could also bind the update to an event triggered by a user and have the user control the visualization. The options are endless.

The exit() function

We've discussed `enter()` and `update`. We've seen how one determines the starting point of our visualization and the other modifies its attributes based on new data coming in. However, the examples covered had the exact number of data elements with the same properties. What would happen if our new dataset had a different amount of items? What if it has fewer or more?

Let's take the `update` part of the previous example and modify it a bit to demonstrate what we're talking about (`http://localhost:8080/chapter-3/example-5.html`):

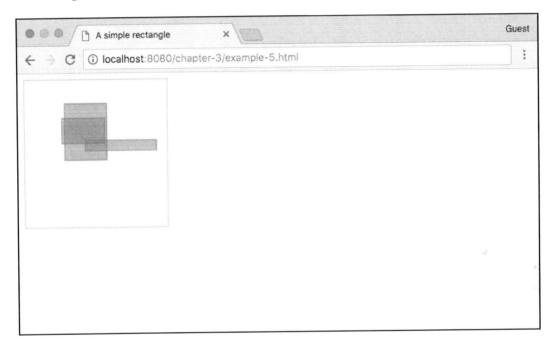

We can explain how this works with two small changes to the `rectangles` function:

```
var rectangles = function(svg) {
  var data = makeData((Math.random() * 5) + 1);
```

Here, we tell the `data` function to create a random number of `data` objects:

```
var rect = svg.selectAll('rect').data(data);

// Enter
rect.enter().append('rect')
  .attr('test', function(d,i) {
```

```
    // Enter called 2 times only
    console.log('enter placing inital rectangle: ', i)
});

// Update
rect.transition().duration(500).attr('x', function(d){ return d.x; })
    .attr('y', function(d){ return d.y; })
    .attr('width', function(d){ return d.width; })
    .attr('height', function(d){ return d.height; })
    .attr('test', function(d, i) {
      // update every data change
      console.log('updating x position to: ', d.x)
    });
```

The exit() function will be the same as before. Add a new exit() section:

```
// Exit
rect.exit().attr('test', function(d) {
  console.log('no data...')
}).remove();
}
```

The exit() method serves the purpose of cleansing or cleaning the no-longer-used DOM items in our visualization. This is helpful because it allows us to join our data with DOM elements, keeping them in sync. An easy way to remember this is as follows: if there are more data elements than DOM elements, the enter() section will be invoked; if there are fewer data elements than DOM elements, the exit() section will be invoked. In the previous example, we just removed the DOM element if there was no matching data.

The following is a graphical representation of the sequence that occurs when enter() and update functions are called. Notice that there's no DOM element for data element 6, so, the enter() section is executed. For data elements 0 to 5, the update code is always called. For data element 6, the **update** section will be executed after the **enter** process has completed. Refer to the following diagram:

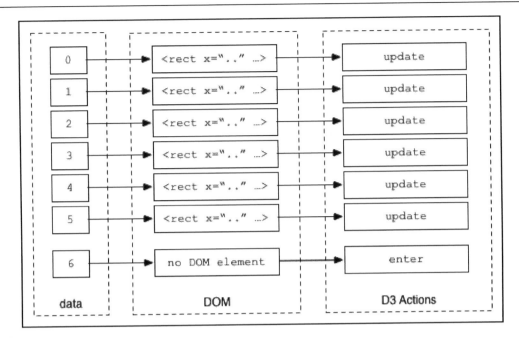

This illustrates what happens when you have fewer data elements than DOM elements. The **update** section is always called where there is a match, as shown in the following diagram:

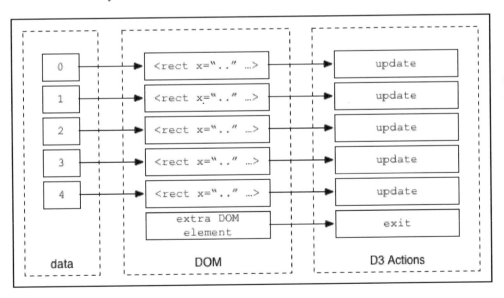

AJAX

Asynchronous JavaScript and XML (AJAX) doesn't relate 100 percent to D3. It actually has its foundation in JavaScript. In short, AJAX allows the developer to obtain data from the background of the web page. This technique is extremely useful in map development because geographic datasets can be very large. Acquiring the data from the background will help produce a refined user experience. In addition, in Chapter 6, *Finding and Working with Geographic Data*, we will cover techniques to compress the size of geographic data.

Separating the data from the code base will also provide the following advantages:

- A lighter code base that is easier to manage
- The ability to update the data without making code changes
- The ability to use third-party providers for data sources

This is accomplished by acquiring the data through an AJAX call with the aid of a D3 function. Let's examine the following code:

```
d3.json("data/dataFile.json", function(error, json) {
```

The d3.json() method has two parameters: a path to the file and a callback function. The callback function indicates what to do with the data once it has been transferred. In the previous code, if the call fetches the data correctly, it assigns it to the json variable. The error variable is just a general error object that indicates whether there were any problems fetching the data or not:

```
if (error) return console.log(error);
var data = json;
```

We store our JSON data into the data variable, and continue to process it as we did in the previous examples:

```
var svg = d3.select("body")
    .append("svg")
    .attr("width", 200)
    .attr("height", 200);

svg.selectAll('rect')
    .data(data).enter()
    .append('rect')
    .attr('x', function(d){ return d.x; })
    .attr('y', function(d){ return d.y; })
    .attr("width", function(d){ return d.width; })
    .attr("height", function(d){ return d.height; });
});
```

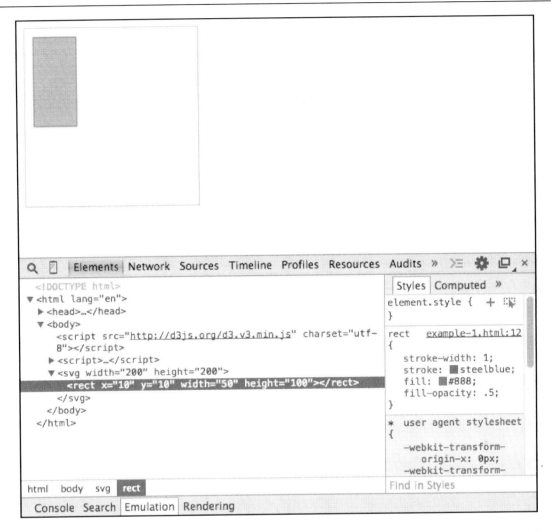

D3 provides us with many kinds of data acquisition methods, and JSON is just one type. It also supports CSV files, plain text files, XML files, or even entire HTML pages. We strongly suggest that you read about AJAX in the documentation
at: `https://github.com/d3/d3/blob/master/API.md#requests-d3-request.`

Summary

In this chapter, we explained the core elements of D3 (`enter()`, `update`, and `exit()`). We understood the power of joining data to our visualization. Not only can data come from many different sources, but it is possible to have the visualization automatically updated as well.

Many detailed examples can be found in the D3 Gallery at: `https://github.com/mbostock/d3/wiki/Gallery`.

In the next chapter, we will combine all of these techniques to build our first map from scratch. Get ready!

4
Creating a Map

It's been quite a ride so far. We've gone through all the different aspects that encompass the creation of a map. We've touched on the basics of SVG, JavaScript, and D3. Now, it's time to put all the pieces together and actually have a final deliverable product. In this chapter, we will cover the following topics through a series of experiments:

- Foundation - creating your basic map
- Experiment 1 - adjusting the bounding box
- Experiment 2 - creating choropleths
- Experiment 3 - adding click events to our visualization
- Experiment 4 - using updates and transitions to enhance our visualization
- Experiment 5 - adding points of interest
- Experiment 6 - adding visualizations as a point of interest

Foundation - creating your basic map

In this section, we will walk through the basics of creating a standard map. The example can be viewed by opening the `example-1.html` file of this chapter provided with this book. If you already have the HTTP server running, you can point your browser to `http://localhost:8080/chapter-4/example-1.html`. On the screen is Mexico (Oscar's beloved country)!

Let's walk through the code to get a step-by-step explanation of how to create this map.

The `width` and `height` can be anything you want. Depending on where your map will be visualized (cellphones, tablets, or desktops), you might want to consider providing a different `width` and `height`:

```
var height = 600;
var width = 900;
```

The next variable defines a projection algorithm that allows you to go from a cartographic space (latitude and longitude) to a Cartesian space (*x*, *y*)—basically a mapping of latitude and longitude to coordinates. You can think of a projection as a way to map the three-dimensional globe to a flat plane. There are many kinds of projections, but `geoMercator()` is normally the default value you will use:

```
var projection = d3.geoMercator();
var mexico = void 0;
```

If you were making a map of the USA, you could use a better projection called AlbersUsa. This is to better position Alaska and Hawaii. By creating a `geoMercator()` projection, Alaska would render proportionate to its size, rivaling that of the entire US. The `geoAlbersUsa()` projection grabs Alaska, makes it smaller, and puts it at the bottom of the visualization. The following screenshot is of `geoMercator()`:

This next screenshot is of `geoAlbersUsa()`:

The D3 library currently contains many built-in projection algorithms. An overview of each one can be viewed at `https://github.com/d3/d3-geo/blob/master/README.md#projections`.

Next, we will assign the projection to our `geoPath()` function. This is a special D3 function that will map the JSON-formatted geographic data into SVG paths. The data format that the `geoPath()` function requires is named GeoJSON and will be covered in `Chapter 6`, *Finding and Working with Geographic Data*:

```
var path = d3.geoPath().projection(projection);
var svg = d3.select("#map")
    .append("svg")
    .attr("width", width)
    .attr("height", height);
```

Including the dataset

The necessary data has been provided for you within the `data` folder, with the filename `geo-data.json`:

```
d3.json('geo-data.json', function(data) {
  console.log('mexico', data);
```

We get the data from an AJAX call, as we saw in the previous chapter.

After the data has been collected, we want to draw only those parts of the data that we are interested in. In addition, we want to automatically scale the map to fit the defined height and width of our visualization.

If you look at the console, you'll see that `mexico` has an `objects` property. Nested inside the `objects` property is `MEX_adm1`. This stands for the administrative areas of Mexico. It is important to understand the geographic data you are using, because other data sources might have different names for the administrative areas property:

```
14:48:37.964 mexico                                                    example-1.html:44
  ▼ Object
    ▶ arcs: (1483) [Array(9), Array(8), Array(2), Array(2), Array(2), Array(2), Array(2), Array(2), Array(2), Array(2), Array
    ▼ objects:
      ▼ MEX_adm1:
        ▶ geometries: (32) [{…}, {…}, {…}, {…}, {…}, {…}, {…}, {…}, {…}, {…}, {…}, {…}, {…}, {…}, {…}, {…}, {…}, {…}, {…
          type: "GeometryCollection"
        ▶ __proto__: Object
      ▶ __proto__: Object
    ▶ transform: {scale: Array(2), translate: Array(2)}
      type: "Topology"
    ▶ __proto__: Object
```

Notice that the `MEX_adm1` property contains a `geometries` array with 32 elements. Each of these elements represents a state in Mexico. Use this data to draw the D3 visualization:

```
var states = topojson.feature(data, data.objects.MEX_adm1);
```

Here, we pass all of the administrative areas to the `topojson.feature()` function in order to extract and create an array of GeoJSON objects. The preceding `states` variable now contains the `features` property. This `features` array is a list of 32 GeoJSON elements, each representing the geographic boundaries of a state in Mexico. We will set an initial scale and translation to 1 and `[0,0]` respectively:

```
// Setup the scale and translate
projection.scale(1).translate([0, 0]);
```

This algorithm is quite useful. The bounding box is a spherical box that returns a two-dimensional array of min/max coordinates, inclusive of the geographic data passed:

```
var b = path.bounds(states);
```

To quote the D3 documentation:

> *"The bounding box is represented by a two-dimensional array: [[left, bottom], [right, top]], where left is the minimum longitude, bottom is the minimum latitude, right is maximum longitude, and top is the maximum latitude."*

This is very helpful if you want to programmatically set the scale and translation of the map. In this case, we want the entire country to fit in our `height` and `width`, so we determine the bounding box of every state in the country of Mexico.

The scale is calculated by taking the longest geographic edge of our bounding box and dividing it by the number of pixels of this edge in the visualization:

```
var s = .95 / Math.max((b[1][0] - b[0][0]) / width, (b[1][1] -
b[0][1]) / height);
```

This can be calculated by first computing the scale of the `width`, then the scale of the `height`, and, finally, taking the larger of the two. All of the logic is compressed into the single line given earlier. The three steps are explained in the following image:

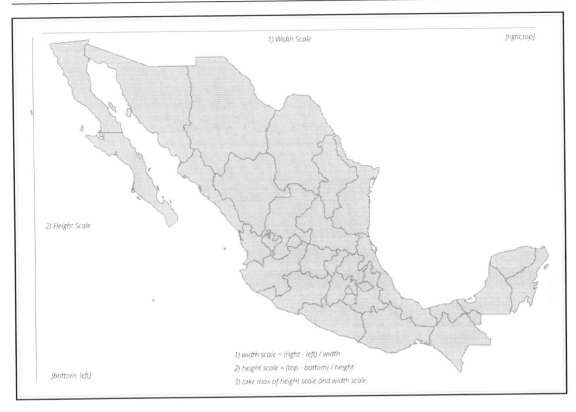

The 95 value adjusts the scale because we are giving the map a bit of a breather at the edges in order to not have the paths intersect the edges of the SVG container item, basically reducing the scale by 5%.

Now, we have an accurate scale of our map, given our set `width` and `height`:

```
var t = [(width - s * (b[1][0] + b[0][0])) / 2, (height - s *
   (b[1][1] + b[0][1])) / 2];
```

As we saw in `Chapter 2`, *Creating Images from Simple Text*, when we scale in SVG, it scales all the attributes (even *x* and *y*). In order to return the map to the center of the screen, we will use the `translate()` function.

The `translate()` function receives an array with two parameters: the amount to translate in *x*, and the amount to translate in *y*. We will calculate *x* by finding the center *(topRight - topLeft)/2* and multiplying it by the scale. The result is then subtracted from the width of the SVG element.

Our *y* translation is calculated similarly but using the *bottomRight - bottomLeft* values divided by 2, multiplied by the scale, then subtracted from the `height`.

Finally, we will reset the projection to use our new scale and translation:

```
projection.scale(s).translate(t);
```

Here, we will create a map variable that will group all of the following SVG elements into a <g> SVG tag. This will allow us to apply styles and better contain all of the proceeding paths' elements:

```
var map = svg.append('g').attr('class', 'boundary');
```

Finally, we are back to the classic D3 enter, update, and exit pattern. We have our data, the list of Mexico states, and we will join this data to the `path` SVG element:

```
mexico = map.selectAll('path').data(states.features);

//Enter
mexico.enter()
    .append('path')
    .attr('d', path);
```

The `Enter` section and the corresponding `path` functions are executed on every data element in the array. As a refresher, each element in the array represents a state in Mexico. The `path` function has been set up to correctly draw the outline of each state, as well as scale and translate it to fit in our SVG container.

Congratulations! You have created your first map!

Experiment 1 – adjusting the bounding box

Now that we have our foundation, let's start with our first experiment. For this experiment, we will manually zoom into a state of Mexico using what we learned in the previous section. The code can be found in `example-2.html` (`http://localhost:8080/chapter-4/example-2.html`); however, feel free to edit `example-1.html` to learn as you go.

For this experiment, we will modify one line of code:

```
var b = path.bounds(states.features[5]);
```

Here, we are telling the calculation to create a boundary based on the sixth element of the `features` array instead of every state in the country of Mexico. The boundaries data will now run through the rest of the scaling and translation algorithms to adjust the map to the one shown in the following screenshot:

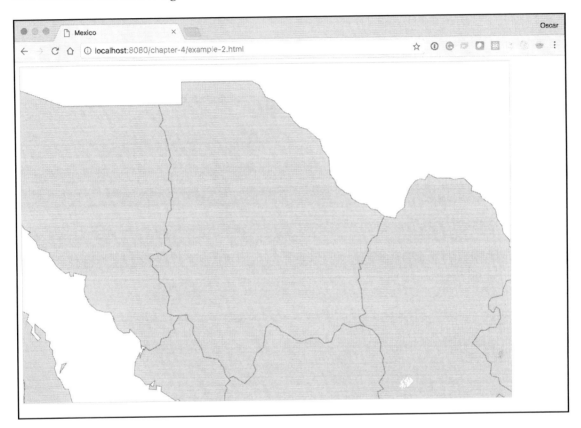

We have basically reduced the min/max of the boundary box to include the geographic coordinates for one state in Mexico (see the next screenshot), and D3 has scaled and translated this information for us automatically:

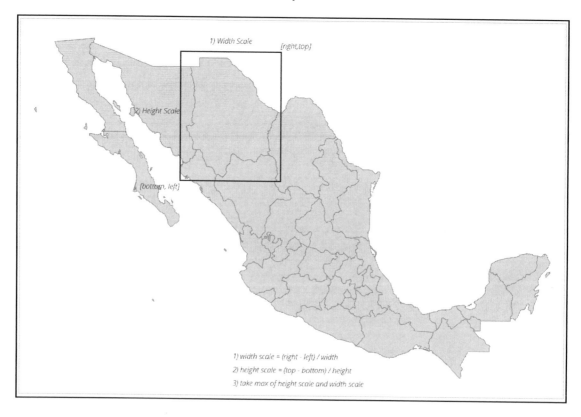

This can be very useful in situations where you might not have the data that you need in isolation from the surrounding areas. Hence, you can always zoom into your geography of interest and isolate it from the rest.

Experiment 2 – creating choropleths

One of the most common uses of D3.js maps is to make choropleths. This visualization gives you the ability to discern between regions, giving them a different color. Normally, this color is associated with some other value, for instance, levels of influenza or a company's sales. The Choropleths are very easy to make in D3.js. In this experiment, we will create a quick choropleth based on the index value of the state in the array of all the states. Look at the following code, or use your browser and go here:

```
http://localhost:8080/chapter-4/example-3.html.
```

We will only need to modify two lines of code in the Update section of our D3 code. Right after the enter() section, add the following two lines:

```
//Update
var color = d3.scaleLinear().domain([0,33]).range(['red',
  'yellow']);
//Enter
mexico.enter()
          .append('path')
          .attr('d', path)
          .attr('fill', function(d,i){
           return color(i);
          });
```

The color variable uses another valuable D3 function named scale. Scales are extremely powerful when creating visualizations in D3; much more detail on scales can be found at:

```
https://github.com/d3/d3/blob/master/API.md#scales-d3-scale.
```

For now, let's describe what this scale defines. Here, we created a new function called color(). This color() function looks for any number between 0 and 33 in an input domain. D3 linearly maps these input values to a color between red and yellow in the output range. D3 has included the capability to automatically map colors in a linear range to a gradient. This means that executing the new function, color, with 0 will return the color red, color(15) will return an orange color, and color(33) will return yellow.

Here is a small table just for visual reference. It shows the color and its respective RGB value:

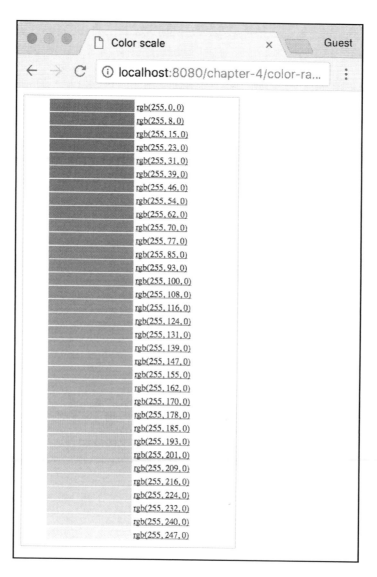

Now, in the update section, we will set the `fill` property of the path to the new `color()` function. This will provide a linear scale of colors and use the index value `i` to determine what color should be returned.

If the color was determined by a different value of the datum, for instance `d.scales`, then you would have a choropleth where the colors actually represent sales. The preceding code should render something as follows:

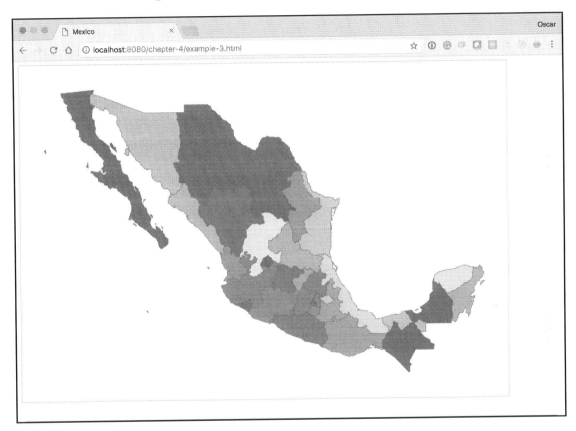

Experiment 3 – adding click events to our visualization

We've seen how to make a map and set different colors to the different regions of this map. Next, we will add a little bit of interactivity. This will illustrate a simple reference to bind click events to maps. For this experiment, we will build on the previous exercise, `example-3.html`. You can see the completed experiment at: `http://localhost:8080/chapter-4/example-4.html`.

First, we need a quick reference to each state in the country. To accomplish this, we will create a new function called `geoID` right below the `mexico` variable:

```
var height = 600;
var width = 900;
var projection = d3.geoMercator();
var mexico = void 0;

var geoID = function(d) {
  return "c" + d.properties.ID_1;
};
```

This function takes in a `state` data element and generates a new selectable ID based on the `ID_1` property found in the data. The `ID_1` property contains a unique numeric value for every state in the array. If we insert this as an `id` attribute into the DOM, then we would create a quick and easy way to select each state in the country.

The following is the `geoID()` function, creating another function called `click`:

```
var click = function(d) {
  d3.selectAll('path').attr('fill-opacity',0.2)
  d3.select('#' + geoID(d)).attr('fill-opacity', 1);
};
```

This method makes it easy to separate what the `click` is doing. The `click` method receives the datum and changes the fill opacity value of all the states to `0.2`. This is done so that when you click on one state and then on the other, the previous state does not maintain the *clicked* style. Notice that the function call is iterating through all the elements of the DOM using the D3 update pattern. After making all the states transparent, we will set a fill opacity of 1 for the given clicked item. This removes all the transparent styling from the selected state. Notice that we are reusing the `geoID()` function that we created earlier to quickly find the state element in the DOM.

Next, let's update the `enter()` method to bind our new `click` method to every new DOM element that `enter()` appends:

```
//Enter
mexico.enter()
    .append('path')
    .attr('d', path)
    .attr('id', geoID)
    .on("click", click)
    .attr('fill', function(d,i) { return color(i); })
```

We also added an attribute called `id`; this inserts the results of the `geoID()` function into the `id` attribute. Again, this makes it very easy to find the clicked state.

The code base should produce a map as follows. Check it out and make sure that you click on any of the states. You will see its color turn a little brighter than the surrounding states:

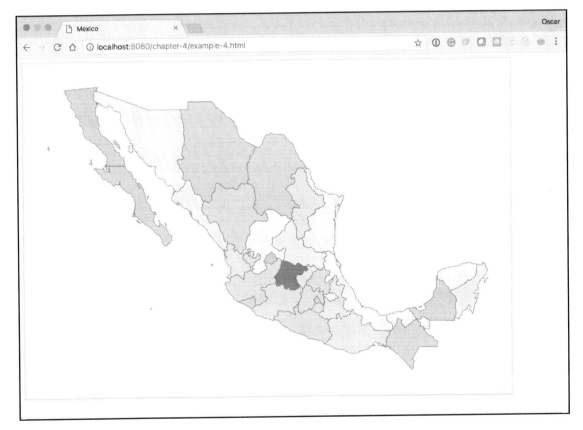

Experiment 4 – using updates and transitions to enhance our visualization

For our next experiment, we will take all of our combined knowledge and add some smooth transitions to the map. Transitions are a fantastic way to add style and smoothness to data changes.

This experiment will, again, require us to start with `example-3.html`. The complete experiment can be viewed at `http://localhost:8080/chapter-4/example-5.html`.

If you remember, we leveraged the JavaScript `setInterval()` function to execute updates at a regular timed frequency. We will go back to this method now to assign a random number between 1 and 33 to our existing `color()` function. We will then leverage a D3 method to smoothly transition between the random color changes.

Right below the update section, add the following `setInterval()` block of code:

```
setInterval(function(){
  map.selectAll('path').transition().duration(500)
      .attr('fill', function(d) {
        return color(Math.floor((Math.random() * 32) + 1));
      });
},2000);
```

This method indicates that, for every 2000 milliseconds (2 seconds), the `map` update section should be executed and the color set to a random number between 1 and 32. The new `transition` and `duration` methods transition from the previous state to the new state over 500 milliseconds. Open `example-5.html` in your browser and you should see the initial color based on the index of the state. After 2 seconds, the colors should smoothly transition to new values.

Experiment 5 – adding points of interest

So far, everything we have done has involved working directly with the geographic data and map. However, there are many cases where you will need to layer additional data on top of the map. We will begin slowly by first adding a few cities of interest to the map of Mexico.

This experiment will, again, require us to start with `example-3.html`. The complete experiment can be viewed at: `http://localhost:8080/chapter-4/example-6.html`.

In this experiment, we will add a `text` element to the page to identify the city. To make the text more visually appealing, we will first add some simple styling in the `<style>` section:

```
text{
   font-family: Helvetica;
   font-weight: 300;
   font-size: 12px;
}
```

Next, we need some data that will indicate the city name, the latitude, and longitude coordinates. For the sake of simplicity, we have added a file with a few starter cities. The file called `cities.csv` is in the same directory as the examples:

```
name,lat,lon,
Cancun,21.1606,-86.8475
Mexico City,19.4333,-99.1333
Monterrey,25.6667,-100.3000
Hermosillo,29.0989,-110.9542
```

Now, add a few lines of code to bring in the data and plot the city locations and names on your map. Add the following block of code right below the exit section (if you are starting with `example-2.html`):

```
d3.csv('cities.csv', function(cities) {
   var cityPoints = svg.selectAll('circle').data(cities);
   var cityText = svg.selectAll('text').data(cities);

   cityPoints.enter()
       .append('circle')
       .attr('cx', function(d) {
          return projection ([d.lon, d.lat])[0]
       })
       .attr('cy', function(d) {
          return projection ([d.lon, d.lat])[1]
       })
       .attr('r', 4)
       .attr('fill', 'steelblue');

   cityText.enter()
       .append('text')
       .attr('x', function(d) {
          return projection([d.lon, d.lat])[0]})
       .attr('y', function(d) {
          return projection([d.lon, d.lat])[1]})
```

```
                    .attr('dx', 5)
                    .attr('dy', 3)
                    .text(function(d) {return d.name});
        });
```

Let's review what we just added.

The d3.csv function will make an AJAX call to our data file and automatically format the entire file into an array of JSON objects. Each property of the object will take on the corresponding name of the column in the .csv file. For example, take a look at the following lines of code:

```
[{
   "name": "Cancun",
   "lat":"21.1606",
   "lon":"-86.8475"
}, ...]
```

Next, we define two variables to hold our data join to the circle and text the SVG elements.

Finally, we will execute a typical enter pattern to place the points as circles and the names as text SVG tags on the map. The *x* and *y* coordinates are determined by calling our previous projection() function with the corresponding latitude and longitude coordinates from the data file.

Note that the projection() function returns an array of *x* and *y* coordinates (*x, y*). The *x* coordinate is determined by taking the 0 index of the returned array. The *y* coordinate is determined from the index, 1. For example, take a look at the following code:

```
   .attr('cx', function(d) {return projection([d.lon, d.lat])[0]})
```

Here, [0] indicates the *x* coordinate.

Your new map should look like the one shown in the following screenshot:

Experiment 6 – adding visualizations as a point of interest

For our final experiment, we will layer visualizations on top of visualizations! Starting from where we left off at http://localhost:8080/chapter-4/example-6.html, we will add a fictitious column to the data to indicate a metric of tequila consumption (the final version can be seen at http://localhost:8080/chapter-4/example-7.html):

```
name,lat,lon,tequila
Cancun,21.1606,-86.8475,85,15
Mexico City,19.4333,-99.1333,51,49
Monterrey,25.6667,-100.3000,30,70
Hermosillo,29.0989,-110.9542,20,80
```

With just two more lines of code, we can have the city points portray meaning. In this experiment, we will scale the radius of the city circles in relation to the amount of tequila consumed:

```
var radius = d3.scaleLinear().domain([0,100]).range([5,30]);
```

Here, we will introduce a new scale that linearly distributes the input values from 1 to 100 to a radius length between 5 and 30. This means that the minimum radius of a circle will be 5 and the maximum will be 30, preventing the circles from growing too large or too small to be readable:

```
cityPoints.enter()
        .append('circle')
        .attr('cx', function(d) {
            return projection([d.lon, d.lat])[0];})
        .attr('cy', function(d) {
            return projection([d.lon, d.lat])[1];})
        .attr('r', 4)
        .attr('fill', 'steelblue');
```

Next, we will change the preceding line of code to call the radius function instead of the hardcoded value of 4. The code will now look like this:

```
.attr('r', function(d) {return radius(d.tequila); })
```

After these two small additions, your map should look like the one shown in the following screenshot:

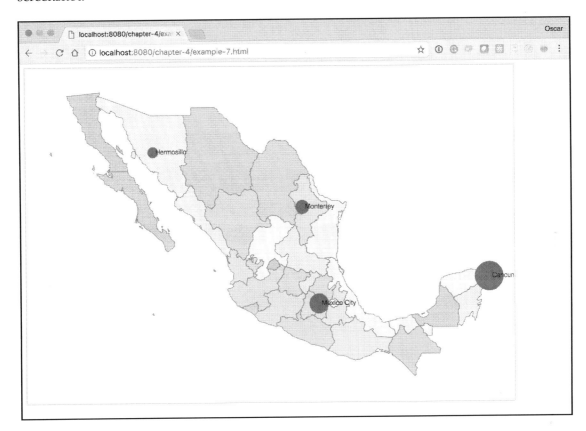

Summary

You learned how to build many different kinds of maps that cover different kinds of needs. The choropleths and data visualizations of maps are some of the most common geographic-based data representations that you will come across. We also added interactivity to our map through basic transitions and events. You will easily realize that, with all the information you've gathered so far, you can independently create engaging map visualizations. You can expand your knowledge by learning advanced interactivity techniques in the next chapter.

Hang on tight!

5
Click-Click Boom! Applying Interactivity to Your Map

In the previous chapter, you learned what is needed to build a basic map with D3.js. We also discussed the concepts of enter, update, and exit and how they apply to maps. You should also understand how D3 mixes and matches HTML with data. However, let's say you want to take it a step further and add more interactivity to your map. We covered only the tip of the iceberg regarding click events in the previous chapter. Now, it's time to dig deeper.

In this chapter, we will expand our knowledge of events and event types. We will progress by experimenting and building upon what you've learned. The following topics are covered in this chapter:

- Events and how they occur
- Experiment 1 - hover events and tooltips
- Experiment 2 - tooltips with visualizations
- Experiment 3 - panning and zooming
- Experiment 4 - orthographic projections
- Experiment 5 - rotating orthographic projections
- Experiment 6 - dragging orthographic projections

Events and how they occur

The following is taken directly from the w3 specifications:

> "The Event interface is used to provide contextual information about an event to the handler processing the event. An object that implements the Event interface is generally passed as the first parameter to an event handler. More specific context information is passed to event handlers by deriving additional interfaces from Event which contain information directly relating to the type of event they accompany. These derived interfaces are also implemented by the object passed to the event listener."

In other words, an event is a user input action that takes place in the browser. If your user clicks, touches, drags, or rotates, an event will fire. If you have event listeners registered to those particular events, the listeners will catch the event and determine the event type. The listeners will also expose properties associated with the event. For example, if we want to add an event listener in plain JavaScript, we would add the following lines of code:

```
<body>
  <button id="btn">Click me</button>

  <script>
    varbtn = document.getElementById('btn');
    btn.addEventListener('click', function() {
      console.log('Hello world'); }, false );
  </script>
</body>
```

Note that you first need to have the button in the DOM in order to get its ID. Once you have it, you can simply add an event listener to listen to the element's click event. The event listener will catch the click event every time it fires and logs `Hello world` to the console.

Until jQuery, events were very tricky, and different browsers had different ways of catching these events. However, thankfully, this is all in the past. Now, we live in a world where modern browsers are more consistent with event handling.

In the world of D3, you won't have to worry about this. Generating events, catching them, and reacting to them is baked into the library and works across all browsers. A good example of this is the hover event.

Experiment 1 – hover events and tooltips

Building on our previous example, we can easily swap our `click` method with a `hover` method. Instead of having `var click`, we will now have `var hover` with the corresponding function. Feel free to open `example-1.html` of the `chapter-5` code base to go over the complete example (`http://localhost:8080/chapter-5/example-1.html`). Let's review the necessary code to change our click event to a hover event. In this particular case, we will need a little more CSS and HTML. In our `<style>` tag, add the following lines:

```
#tooltip{
position: absolute;
z-index: 2;
background: rgba(0,153,76,0.8);
width:130px;
height:20px;
color:white;
font-size: 14px;
padding:5px;
top:-150px;
left:-150px;
font-family: "HelveticaNeue-Light", "Helvetica Neue Light",
  "Helvetica Neue", Helvetica, Arial, "Lucida Grande", sans-serif;
}
```

This style is for a basic tooltip. It is positioned **absolutely** so that it can take whatever x and y coordinates we give it (left and top). It also has some filler styles for the fonts and colors. The `tooltip` is styled to the element in the DOM that has the ID of #`tooltip`:

```
<div id="tooltip"></div>
```

Next, we add the logic to handle a `hover` event when it is fired:

```
var hover = function(d) {
  var div = document.getElementById('tooltip');
  div.style.left = event.pageX +'px';
  div.style.top = event.pageY + 'px';
  div.innerHTML = d.properties.NAME_1;
};
```

This function, aside from logging the event, will find the DOM element with an ID of `tooltip` and position it at the *x* and *y* coordinates of the event. These coordinates are a part of the properties of the event and are named `pageX` and `pageY`, respectively. Next, we will insert text with the state name (`d.properties.NAME_1`) into the `tooltip`:

```
//Enter
mexico.enter()
   .append('path')
   .attr('d', path)
   .on("mouseover", hover);
```

Finally, we will change our binding from a click to a `mouseover` event in the on section of the code. We will also change the event handler to the `hover` function we created earlier.

Once the changes have been saved and viewed, you should notice basic tooltips on your map:

Experiment 2 – tooltips with visualizations

In this next experiment, we will enhance our tooltips with additional visualizations. In a similar fashion, we will outline the additional code to provide this functionality (`http://localhost:8080/chapter-5/example-2.html`).

To our CSS, we will need to add the following lines of code:

```
#tooltip svg{
border-top:0;
margin-left:-5px;
margin-top:7px;
}
```

This will style our SVG container (inside our tooltip DOM element) to align it with the label of the state.

Next, we'll include two new scripts to create visualizations:

```
<script src="base.js"></script>
<script src="sparkline.js"></script>
```

The preceding JavaScript files contain the D3 code for creating a line chart visualization. The chart itself contains and leverages the *Towards Reusable Chart* described by Mike Bostock at: `http://bost.ocks.org/mike/chart/`. Feel free to examine the code; it is a very simple visualization that follows the enter, update, and exit pattern. We will explore this chart further in Chapter 7, *Testing*:

```
var db = d3.map();
var sparkline = d3.charts.sparkline().height(50).width(138);
```

We will now declare two new variables. The `db` variable will hold a hashmap to quickly lookup values by `geoID`. The `sparkline` variable is the function that will draw our simple line chart:

```
var setDb = function(data) {
  data.forEach(function(d) {
    db.set(d.geoID, [
        {"x": 1, "y": +d.q1},
        {"x": 2, "y": +d.q2},
        {"x": 3, "y": +d.q3},
        {"x": 4, "y": +d.q4}
    ]);
  });
};
```

This function parses data and formats it into a structure that the `sparkline` function can use to create the line chart:

```
var geoID = function(d) {
  return "c" + d.properties.ID_1;
};
```

We will bring back our `geoID` function from Chapter 4, *Creating a Map*, in order to quickly create unique IDs for each state:

```
var hover = function(d) {
  var div = document.getElementById('tooltip');
  div.style.left = event.pageX +'px';
  div.style.top = event.pageY + 'px';
  div.innerHTML = d.properties.NAME_1;

  var id = geoID(d);
  d3.select("#tooltip").datum(db.get(id)).call(sparkline.draw);
};
```

For our hover event handler, we need to add two new lines. First, we will declare an ID variable that holds the unique `geoID` for the state we are hovering over. Then, we will call our `sparkline` function to draw a line chart in the `tooltip` selection. The data is retrieved from the preceding db variable. For more information on how the call works, refer to: `https://developer.mozilla.org/en-US/docs/Web/JavaScript/Reference/Global_Obj ects/Function/call`:

```
d3.csv('states-data.csv', function(data) {
  setDb(data);
});
```

We load our `.csv` file via AJAX and invoke the `setDb()` function (described earlier).

You should now see a map that displays a `tooltip` with a line chart for every state in Mexico. In summary:

1. The map is drawn as usual.
2. We will create a small lookup db that contains additional data about each state.
3. Then, we will register a hover event that fires whenever the user's mouse passes over a state.
4. The hover event fires and retrieves data about the state.
5. The hover event also places the name of the state in the DOM and calls a function that creates a line chart with the retrieved data:

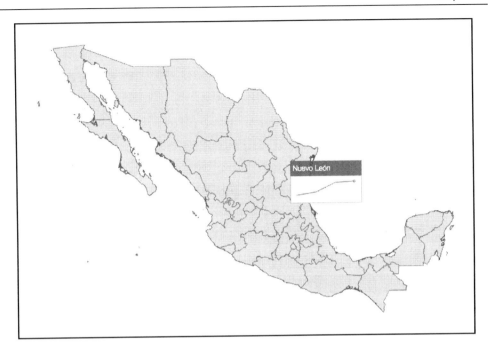

Experiment 3 – panning and zooming

A very common request when working with maps is to provide the ability to pan and zoom around the visualization. This is especially useful when a large map contains abundant detail. Luckily, D3 provides an event listener to help with this feature. In this experiment, we will outline the principles to provide basic panning and zooming for your map. This experiment requires us to start with `example-1.html`; however, feel free to look at `http://localhost:8080/chapter-5/example-3.html` for reference.

First, we will add a simple CSS class in our `<style>` section; this class will act as a rectangle over the entire map. This will be our zoomable area:

```
.overlay {
fill: none;
pointer-events: all;
}
```

Next, we need to define a function to handle the event when the zoom listener is fired. The following function can be placed right below the map declaration:

```
var zoomed = function () {
  map.attr("transform", "translate("+ d3.event.translate + ")
    scale(" + d3.event.scale + ")");
};
```

This function takes advantage of two variables exposed while panning and zooming: `d3.event.scale` and `d3.event.translate`. The variables are defined as follows:

- `d3.event.scale`: This defines the zoom level in terms of an SVG scale.
- `d3.event.translate`: This defines the position of the map in relation to the mouse in terms of an SVG translate.

With this information available, we can set the SVG attributes (scale and translate) of the map container to the event variables:

```
var zoom = d3.behavior.zoom()
    .scaleExtent([1, 8])
    .on("zoom", zoomed);
    .size([width, height]);
```

Similar to the hover event listener, we need to create a new zoom event listener. Create the preceding function after the `zoom()` function. Note that there is one additional setting to understand, `scaleExtent()`.

The `scaleExtent()` setting provides a scale range of the zooming amount. The first element in the array is the maximum that the map can zoom out. The second element in the array is the maximum that the map can zoom in. Remember that 1 is the original size of our map based on our bounding-box formula from Chapter 4, *Creating a Map*. The minimum value that `scaleExtent()` can be set to is 0, to zoom out. In example-3.html, alter these numbers to get a feel of how they work. For example, if you change 1 to 5, you will see that the map can zoom out to half its original size.

There are additional settings to this event listener that can be reviewed at: https://github.com/mbostock/d3/wiki/Zoom-Behavior:

```
svg.append("rect")
    .attr("class", "overlay")
    .attr("width", width)
    .attr("height", height)
    .call(zoom);
```

Finally, right after the `mexico.exit` section, we will add a transparent rectangle to the entire visualization and bind the new listener. Remember that the rectangle is using the CSS class we defined at the beginning of the experiment.

Now, you should have full zooming and panning capabilities on the Mexican map. You can either double-click to zoom in or use your scroll wheel. The interactions should also work for swipe and pinch gestures on a tablet:

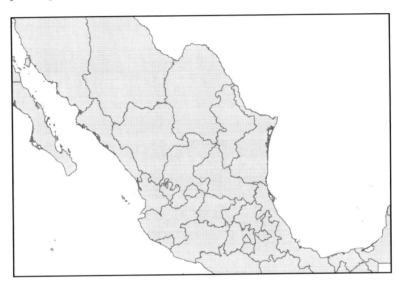

Experiment 4 – orthographic projections

For the next set of experiments in this chapter, we will switch gears and look at interactivity with orthographic projections (representing a three-dimensional map on a two-dimensional screen). A better visualization to illustrate these concepts is the entire globe instead of a single country. This experiment will start with `http://localhost:8080/chapter-5/example-4.html` and require a new datafile, which is provided for you. You will notice that the code base is almost identical, with the exception of three changes that we will outline here:

```
var height = 600;
var width = 900;
var projection = d3.geo.orthographic().clipAngle(90);
var path = d3.geo.path().projection(projection);
```

First, we will change our d3.geo projection from d3.geo.mercator to
d3.geo.orthographic. We also have an additional setting to configure: the clipAngle at
90 degrees. This places an imaginary plane through the globe and clips the back of the
projection:

```
d3.json('world.json', function(data) {
var countries = topojson.feature(data, data.objects.countries);
var map = svg.append('g').attr('class', 'boundary');
var world = map.selectAll('path').data(countries.features);
```

Next, we will substitute the old geo-data.json file for the new datafile, world.json. We
will also set up new variables for our data joining in order to provide better readability in
the code:

```
world.enter()
      .append('path')
      .attr('d', path);
```

As we have seen many times now, we will apply the standard enter() pattern. You should
now have a static map of the globe, as seen in the following screenshot. You can also work
directly with example-4.html.

In the last two sections, we will bring the globe to life!

Experiment 5 – rotating orthographic projections

Our previous example was very fascinating. We went from visualizing a map in two dimensions to three dimensions with just a few lines. The next step is to animate it. For this experiment, open `http://localhost:8080/chapter-5/example-5.html` in the code samples. Let's now piece it together:

```
var i = 0;
```

We added an index variable that will hold the rotation rate. Don't worry; we'll explain how this is used here:

```
d3.json('world.json', function(data) {
var countries = topojson.feature(data, data.objects.countries);
var mexico = countries.features[102];
```

As Mexico is the center of the universe and requires special attention, we isolated it into its own variable by taking the corresponding feature from the countries' feature array. This will allow us to manipulate it separately from the rest of the globe:

```
var map = svg.append('g').attr('class', 'boundary');
var world = map.selectAll('path').data(countries.features);
var mexico = map.selectAll('.mexico').data([mexico]);
```

Next, we will data join the information we isolated earlier to its own variable. This way, we will have one map that represents the entire world and another one that represents just Mexico:

```
mexico.enter()
  .append('path')
  .attr('class', 'mexico')
  .attr('d', path)
  .style('fill', 'lightyellow').style('stroke', 'orange');
```

We will inject the map of Mexico and apply the `geo.path` that contains the same projection we used for the world map. We will also add a light yellow background to Mexico using the `fill` CSS style and an orange border using the stroke:

```
setInterval(function() {
i = i+0.2;
        // move i around in the array to get a feel for yaw, pitch
        // and roll
        // see diagram
projection.rotate([i,0,0])
```

```
world.attr('d', path);
mexico.attr('d', path)
    .style('fill', 'lightyellow').style('stroke', 'orange');
    }, 20);
```

This is where the action starts, literally. We created an interval that executes every 20 milliseconds. This interval contains a function that utilizes our index variable and increments the value by 0.2. This value is then applied to the rotate function of our projection. Specifically, we will adjust the rotation every 20 ms on this line of code:

```
projection.rotate([i,0,0])
```

Yaw is represented by the first value of the array (in this case, i), pitch represented by the second value, and roll by the third value. Yaw, pitch, and roll are rotation angles and are applied in their respective vectors. The following image provides an illustration of how the angles rotate:

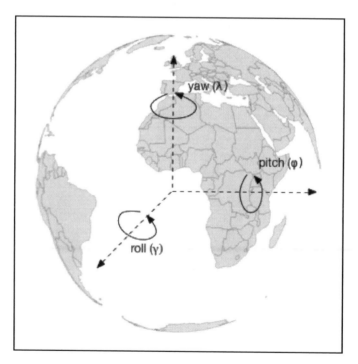

Here, we see that the yaw vector points in the z direction and is around the center axis. The pitch goes along our x axis, and the yaw goes around our y axis. The Greek characters (in parentheses in the preceding image) are often used to depict yaw, pitch, and roll.

In our case, the index variable, `i`, is increasing and is allocated to the yaw rotation. This means that our globe will spin from left to right around the center axis. If we were to swap the position of our index so that it is in the pitch location (the second array element), our globe would spin vertically:

```
project.rotate([0,i,0]);
```

Finally, we will use the same D3 update pattern and update all the paths with the new projection. Give it a shot, play around with the example, and see how the globe spins in different directions. When complete, you will see the rotating globe in your browser, as in the following screenshot:

Experiment 6 – dragging orthographic projections

For our last example, we will add the ability to drag our globe so that the user can spin it to the left or right. Open `http://localhost:8080/chapter-5/example-6.html` from the code samples and let's get started:

```
var dragging = function(d) {
var c = projection.rotate();
projection.rotate([c[0] + d3.event.dx/2, c[1], c[2]])

world.attr('d', path);
mexico.attr('d', path)
        .style('fill', 'lightyellow').style('stroke', 'orange');
};
```

Our first piece of new code is our dragging event handler. This function will be executed every time the user drags the mouse on the screen. The algorithm executes the following steps:

1. Stores the current rotation value.
2. Updates the projection's rotation based on the distance it is dragged.
3. Updates all the paths in the world map.
4. Updates all the paths in the map of Mexico.

The second step deserves a little more explanation. Just like the `d3.behavior.zoom` event handler, `d3.behavior.drag` exposes information about the performed action. In this case, `d3.event.dx` and `d3.event.dy` indicate the distance dragged from the previous location. The `c[0] + d3.event.dx/2` code tells us that we need to take the previous yaw value and add the amount of drag the user is performing. We will divide the drag amount by two to slow down the rotation by half; otherwise, every pixel the user drags will correlate to *1* degree of rotation:

```
var drag = d3.behavior.drag()
    .on("drag", dragging);
```

Next, we will bind our `dragging` method to our drag event, as we saw earlier, with click, hover, and zoom:

```
svg.append("rect")
      .attr("class", "overlay")
      .attr("width", width)
      .attr("height", height)
      .call(drag);
```

Finally, we need an area to bind our drag event. Using our previous technique, we will add a transparent rectangle on top of the visualization. This will allow us to very clearly detect the *x* and *y* positions on our SVG element.

Give it a spin! You'll notice that if you click-and-drag the world, it will spin in the corresponding yaw direction:

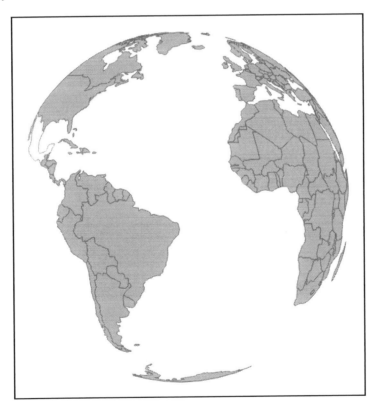

Summary

We covered many examples to get you started with interactivity for your D3 map visualizations. We went over the basics of event handling, explored various methods to bind events to the map, outlined the two d3.behavior APIs, and even dipped our toes into orthographic projections. If you wish to dig deeper into world rotations, and the math involved, check out the Jason Davies article
at: http://www.jasondavies.com/maps/rotate/.

After two chapters of drawing and interacting with maps, the next chapter will explain how to obtain geo data in order to create any map you want. We'll also include some techniques to optimize the data files for viewing the web.

6
Finding and Working with Geographic Data

We have spent a significant amount of time creating and interacting with maps in our previous chapters. In all our examples, the geographic data was included. In this chapter, we will explain how to find geographic data about any country in the world.

There are typically two sets of data that we will need to create a map in D3:

- A dataset that represents the geographic shape of our map (geodata)
- Some meaningful data that we want to visualize on the map (for example, population density by US countries, or unemployment rate by countries in the world)

This chapter is focused on understanding, manipulating, and optimizing geodata for map visualizations. We will accomplish these goals by:

- Explaining three important formats that contain geospatial vector data
- Finding, downloading, and working with large amounts of map data
- Using techniques to build the right geodata file for your map

Geodata file types

There are dozens of file formats that represent geographic information. In this section, we will focus on three file types: shapefiles, GeoJSON, and TopoJSON.

What are shapefiles and how do I get them?

Shapefiles are the most popular vector-based file format. They contain polygons and lines that represent geographic boundaries. The shapefile format was developed by the company Esri as an open standard to work with **geographic information systems (GIS)**. This vector information can also describe other geographic entities (rivers, lakes, and railroads). In addition, the file format has the ability to store data attributes that are useful when working with visualizations (for example, the name of the geographic object, the type, and some relationships). Most importantly for us, there is a large repository of free shapefiles located at `http://diva-gis.org`. This repository contains a tremendous wealth of data at different levels of specificity and granularity.

Unfortunately for us, shapefiles are in binary format and can be very large. This makes them very difficult, if not impossible, to use in standard web development. Thankfully, there are some tools to help us leverage the large repository of shapefiles and convert them to GeoJSON and TopoJSON. GeoJSON and TopoJSON are JavaScript-friendly, much smaller, and easier to use in our web development context. In the previous chapters, all of the geographic data was provided in TopoJSON.

Acquiring shapefiles for a specific country

Let's start with a map of Spain and go through the process of getting our first shapefile:

1. Go to `http://www.diva-gis.org/gdata` and select **Spain** from the drop-down list, as shown in the following screenshot:

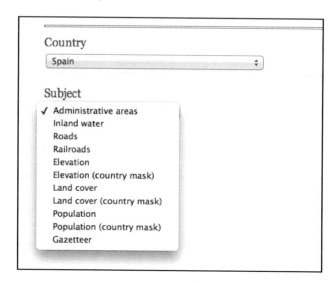

1. Once **Spain** is selected, you will see a large selection of geographic data to choose from (**Roads**, **Railroads**, and so on). Select the **Administrative areas** option to draw the primary boundaries of the country and regions. Click on **OK**; it will take you to the download page.

2. Once it's downloaded, you will have an `ESP_adm.zip` file containing the shapefile data for the administrative areas of Spain.

3. After unzipping the file, you will see that the files are organized into progressively increasing numbers, `ESP_adm0` to `ESP_adm4`. ESP represents the abbreviation of the country and each number represents the increasing amount of detail found in each data file. For example, `ESP_adm0` will draw just the outline of Spain, while `ESP_adm3` will include the provinces of the country.

GeoJSON

GeoJSON is a specific JSON format for describing geographic data structures. It is important to know that GeoJSON does the following:

- Contains all the information required to draw geographic data.
- Is a standard JSON format and can be used instantly in JavaScript when building for the web.
- Is required by D3 when defining our `d3.geo.path` function, as seen in the previous chapters.
- Discretely defines each geographic shape. For example, if two countries share a border, the GeoJSON file will completely define both countries, therefore defining the border twice. It does not provide any mechanisms to optimize the data file.

Because D3 relies on GeoJSON, we will explain some of the highlights of the specification. For a complete explanation, please see `http://geojson.org`.

Typically, you will not incorporate the GeoJSON file directly in your D3 work. TopoJSON, explained in the next section, offers a more compact solution. However, it is still important to understand the specification, so let's walk through the GeoJSON of Spain:

```
{
    "type": "FeatureCollection",
    "features": [
        {
```

```
        "type": "Feature",
        "properties": {
            "GADMID": 70,
            "ISO": "ESP",
            "NAME_ENGLI": "Spain",
            "NAME_ISO": "SPAIN",
            "NAME_FAO": "Spain",
            "NAME_LOCAL": "España",
            ...
        },
        "geometry": {
            "type": "MultiPolygon",
            "coordinates": [
                [
                    [
                        [
                            0.518472,
                            40.53236
                        ],
                        [
                            0.518194,
                            40.53236
                        ],
                        ...
                    ]
                ]
            ]
        }
    }
]
}
```

The first property of the JSON object identifies the GeoJSON file as a collection of features
(FeatureCollection). Each member of the collection (the array in the preceding
features property) holds a specially formatted JSON object called a feature. The
d3.geo.path function that we used in the previous chapters knows how to convert the
feature object into a polygon using an SVG path. By iterating over an array of these
features and drawing each polygon one by one, we create a D3 map.

The `feature` object must adhere to the following properties in order for D3 to convert the object into a polygon:

- `geometry`: This is another GeoJSON specification that contains types and coordinates that indicate exactly how to draw the shape. We will not spend a lot of time explaining exactly how the specification draws the object. D3 will do all the hard work for us. Leveraging the enter/update/exit pattern, we pass a special `d3.geo.path` function to each feature. This function will take the geometry information about the feature and create the shape for us automatically.

- `properties`: This is any additional data to be attached to the feature. This is a typical name/value pair JSON object. In the preceding example, the `properties` attribute is leveraged to store the name of the country. This is very helpful when we need to find the country later to bind additional data to the visualization. See the following screenshot for examples of properties that can be bound to a feature object:

```
▼ 1: Object
  ▶ geometry: Object
  ▼ properties: Object
      CC_1: "02"
      ENGTYPE_1: "Autonomous Community"
      HASC_1: "ES.AR"
      ID_0: 70
      ID_1: 936
      ISO: "ESP"
      NAME_0: "Spain"
      NAME_1: "Aragón"
      NL_NAME_1: null
      REMARKS_1: null
      Shape_Area: 5.15083538648
      Shape_Leng: 15.0953070773
      TYPE_1: "Comunidad Autónoma"
      VALIDFR_1: "1982"
      VALIDTO_1: "Present"
      VARNAME_1: "Aragão|Aragó|Aragón|Aragona|Aragonien"
    ▶ __proto__: Object
    type: "Feature"
  ▶ __proto__ : Object
```

- `id`: This is a placeholder that can be leveraged to store a unique identifier to the particular feature in the collection.

A quick map in D3 with only GeoJSON

For a moment, let's pretend that TopoJSON does not exist and illustrate how only GeoJSON can be used to create a map. This will help illustrate the need for TopoJSON in the next section. The following code snippet is a quick example to tie everything together; you can also open `example-1.html` from the `chapter-6` folder (`http://localhost:8080/chapter-6/example-1.html`) to see the map in your browser of the following code:

```
d3.json('geojson/spain-geo.json', function(data) {
  var b, s, t;
  projection.scale(1).translate([0, 0]);
  var b = path.bounds(data);
  var s = .9 / Math.max((b[1][0] - b[0][0]) / width,
    (b[1][1] - b[0][1]) / height);
    var t = [(width - s * (b[1][0] +
    b[0][0])) / 2,
    (height - s * (b[1][1] + b[0][1])) / 2];
  projection.scale(s).translate(t);

  map = svg.append('g').attr('class', 'boundary');
  spain = map.selectAll('path').data(data.features);
```

Notice that the code is almost identical to the examples in the previous chapters. The only exception is that we are not calling the `topojson` function (we will cover why `topojson` is important next). Instead, we are passing the data from the AJAX call directly into the *data join* for the following `enter()` call:

```
spain.enter()
   .append('path')
   .attr('d', path);

});
```

As predicted, we have our map of Spain:

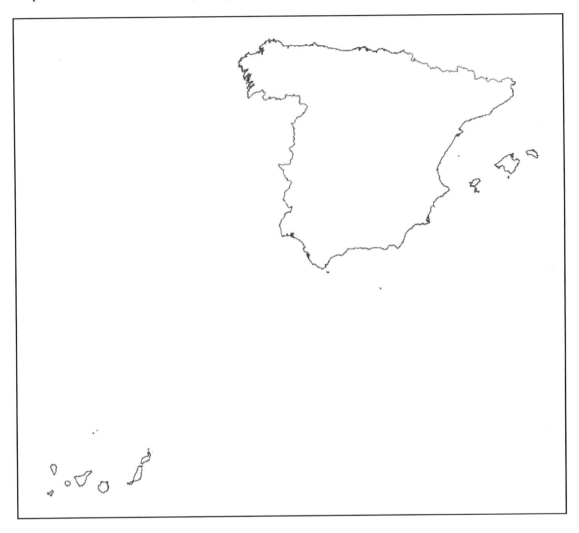

While using GeoJSON directly may seem like the best approach, there are some problems. Primarily, a one-to-one conversion of an Esri shapefile to the GeoJSON format contains a lot of detail that is probably unnecessary and will create a huge GeoJSON file. The larger the file, the more time it will take to download. For example, spain-geo.json produced an almost 7 MB GeoJSON file.

Next, we will explore how TopoJSON can help by modifying several optimization levers while still maintaining significant details.

TopoJSON basics

TopoJSON is another JSON-based format that encodes geographic data. If you remember, GeoJSON describes geographic data discretely. This means GeoJSON borders can be described twice. The TopoJSON format removes this duplicate behavior, often creating files that are 80 percent smaller. This format is extremely helpful when building for the web, where data transfer size plays an important role.

The term TopoJSON can be confusing. Let's break it down into its three dimensions:

- **TopoJSON, the serialized format**: The actual serialized JSON format that describes how to draw geographic shapes.
- **topojson, the command-line utility**: This is a program that a user can run to create TopoJSON files from shapefiles. The utility contains many levers to further reduce the size of the file.
- **topojson.js, the JavaScript library**: The library used in your D3 map to convert the TopoJSON-serialized format back to GeoJSON, so that the d3.geo.path functions work correctly.

To illustrate to what extent TopoJSON can reduce the file size, let's execute the command-line utility against the shapefiles we downloaded earlier. Open the command line and execute the following in the same directory where you downloaded and unzipped the ESP_adm.zip file:

```
topojson -o spain-topo.json -p -- ESP_adm0.shp
```

This command creates a new TopoJSON-formatted file named spain-topo.json and preserves all the data properties (the -p flag) from the ESP_adm0 shapefile (note that the shapefile needs to come after the -- in the command-line syntax). The -o parameter defines the name of the resulting TopoJSON file.

First, let's compare file sizes with GeoJSON versus TopoJSON for the exact same geographic region:

- GeoJSON: 6.4 MB
- TopoJSON: 379 KB

This is an incredible compression rate, and we just used the defaults!

In order to incorporate TopoJSON into our map, we need to use the `topojson.js` JavaScript library and alter a few lines of code. We will start with `example-1.html`. The final version can be viewed in `example-2.html` (`http://localhost:8080/chapter-6/example-2.html`):

```
<script src="http://d3js.org/topojson.v1.min.js"></script>
```

First, we add the JavaScript library as a `<script>` tag to our file. Now you know why we have been using this library all along:

```
d3.json('topojson/spain-topo.json', function(data) {
```

Next, we inject our `topojson` file that we just created via AJAX:

```
var country = topojson.feature(data, data.objects.ESP_adm0);
```

We add an additional line of code to convert the TopoJSON format to the GeoJSON feature format:

```
var b = path.bounds(country);
```

We need to remember to create our bounding box using the interpolated features:

```
spain = map.selectAll('path').data(country.features);
```

Now, we use the *data join* on our new data. As expected, we will see our map of Spain. Let's show them side by side in the following screenshot to compare GeoJSON and TopoJSON (with GeoJSON on the left and TopoJSON on the right):

TopoJSON command-line tips

The TopoJSON command-line documentation is very complete (`https://github.com/mbostock/topojson/wiki/Command-Line-Reference`). However, here are a couple of quick and easy tips to get you started.

Preserving specific attributes

In the GeoJSON section, we illustrated that data properties are often part of the geographic data. The `topojson` command gives you the ability to filter out the ones you are not interested in, as well as provide a better naming convention to the ones you do want to keep. These capabilities are in the `-p` flag and passed to the command. For example:

```
topojson -o spain-topo.json -p name=ISO -- ESP_adm0.shp
```

We will create the TopoJSON file, remove all properties except ISO, and rename the ISO property to something easy to recognize. You can address multiple properties by comma-separating the list:

```
-p target=source,target=source,target=source
```

Simplification

Mike Bostock provides an excellent tutorial on simplification, and how it works, at `http://bost.ocks.org/mike/simplify/`.

Basically, it is a way to reduce geometric complexity through line-simplification algorithms. For example, if you do not need much detail in a very jagged coast of a country, you can apply line-simplification algorithms to smooth out the jaggedness and significantly reduce the size of the TopoJSON file. The command-line parameter you use is `-s` to adjust the simplification in the TopoJSON conversion:

```
-p  name=ISO -s 7e-7 -- ESP_adm0.shp
```

We typically realize that when dealing with shapefiles from DIVA-GIS, the best range is around 7e-7 to keep within the per-pixel threshold, which is less than the area of the map. At this range, the size compression is very significant and the map quality is still very acceptable for web development. Consider the following:

- **Original**: 378 KB, great detail and quality:

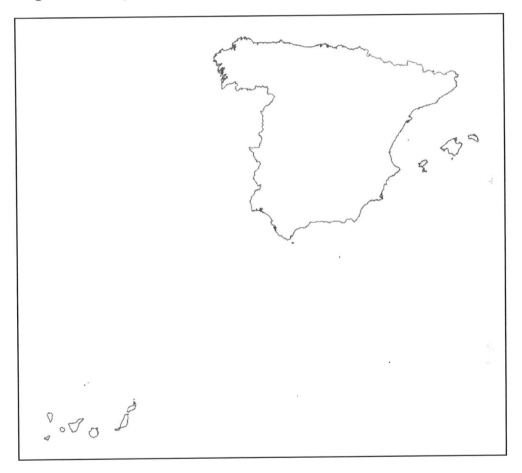

- **Simplified at -s 7e-7**: 3.6 KB and acceptable quality:

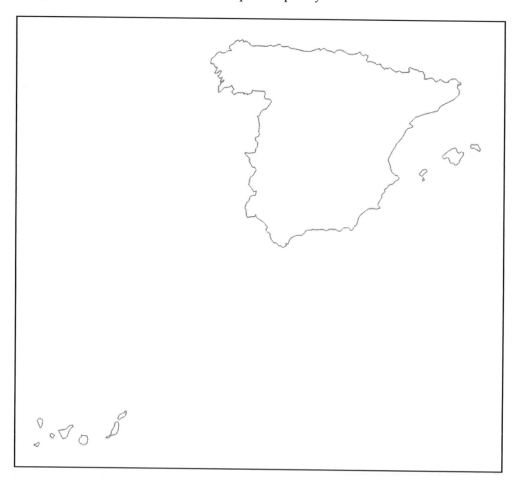

- **Very simple at -s 7e-5**: 568 bytes but the map is unrecognizable:

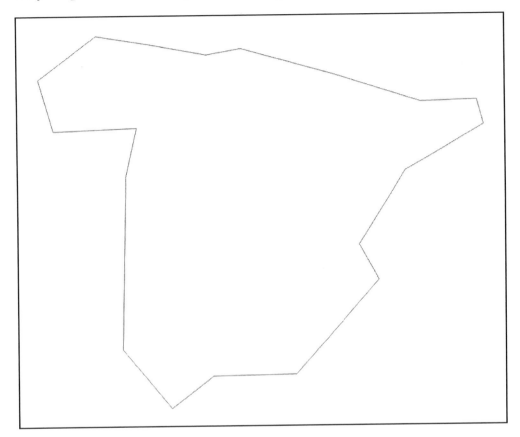

Merging files

The final tip involves merging multiple shapefiles into a single TopoJSON file. This is extremely useful if you need separate geographic information but want to fetch it in a single AJAX request. To append additional files, you add them after the – in the command line. Consider this command:

```
topojson -o ../topojson/spain-topo-simple.json -p  name=ISO -s 7e-7 -
- ESP_adm0.shp ESP_adm1.shp
```

It will produce the following object structure, where the data for `ESP_adm0` is the data for the country, and `ESP_adm1` is the data for the regions:

```
data ▼ Object {type: "Topology", objects: Objec
        ▶ arcs: Array[285]
        ▼ objects: Object
          ▶ ESP_adm0: Object
          ▶ ESP_adm1: Object
          ▶ __proto__: Object
        ▶ transform: Object
          type: "Topology"
        ▶ __proto__: Object
```

There is also the opportunity to rename the object they will map to in the resulting TopoJSON file. Again, this can help create readable code. The renaming follows the same convention as renaming specific properties. For example, type in this command:

```
topojson -o ../topojson/spain-topo-simple.json -p  name=ISO -s 7e-7 -
- country=ESP_adm0.shp regions=ESP_adm1.shp
```

The preceding command will create the following:

```
▼ Object {type: "Topology", objec
  ▶ arcs: Array[285]
  ▼ objects: Object
    ▶ country: Object
    ▶ regions: Object
    ▶ __proto__: Object
  ▶ transform: Object
    type: "Topology"
  ▶ __proto__: Object
```

In this case, you would change your original code, which is as follows:

```
var country = topojson.feature(data, data.objects.ESP_adm0);
```

You have to change it to the following code:

```
var country = topojson.feature(data, data.objects.country);
```

This is much nicer to look at! Please look at `example-3.html` (`http://localhost:8080/chapter-6/example-3.html`) to see how all of this information can be tied together.

Summary

At this point, you should feel confident that you can find and modify datasets to your needs. We've covered common locations from where you can acquire data, and we've touched on the different types of flags TopoJSON offers. With these skills, it is up to you to make sure your data is trimmed and is acquired to your visualization needs. This closes the circle of developing maps with D3. In the next chapter, we will refine your craft by focusing on testing your visualizations.

7
Testing

In this chapter, we will cover several topics that will assist you in the long-term maintenance of your D3 code base. The goal is to create a foundation to build reusable assets that can be easily unit tested while leveraging popular tools and techniques already established in the JavaScript community.

Unit testing is important in any software development project, especially in a D3 code base. Typically, these projects involve a lot of code that applies analytics or manipulates data structures. For these types of problems, unit testing can help in the following ways:

- **Reduce bugs**: An automated test suite will allow the developer to break down and test individual components. These tests will be run constantly throughout the development cycle, validating that future features do not break the older working code.
- **Document accurately**: Often, tests are written in a human-readable way; this precisely describes the problem they are testing against. An example of the code provides much better documentation than a long paragraph.
- **Allow refactoring**: The developer can change code semantics and design with confidence, knowing that the inputs and outputs are still tracked and validated.
- **Make development faster**: Most developers spend time validating their work as they write. We've seen developers tirelessly refresh browsers, check console logs, and inspect DOM elements as they go. Instead of performing these manual actions over and over again, simply wrap them up in a framework that does the work for you.

This chapter will explore a Bootstrap project that we like to use when starting a new visualization development. The concepts covered in the project include:

- Project structure
- Code organization and reusable assets
- Unit testing
- A resilient code base

Code organization and reusable assets

The foundation of our way of writing reusable and testable D3 code is from Mike Bostock's blog article, *Towards Reusable Charts*, at http://bost.ocks.org/mike/chart/. At its core, it sets out to implement charts as closures with getter and setter methods. This makes the code more readable and simple for testing. It is actually a great idea to read this article before continuing, as we can take some of our career experiences and extend these concepts a little further. The project structure is organized to achieve several goals.

Project structure

The Bootstrap project contains the following files and directories:

The project works out of the box with example code already in place. To see this in action, we will launch the example. From the example Bootstrap code provided, first, install all the dependencies (note that you only have to execute this command once):

```
npm install
```

Then, to see the visualization, execute the following:

```
node node_modules/http-server/bin/http-server
```

Next, open the browser to `http://localhost:8080`. You should see three bars changing based on random data in a series of tests. Note that if you have the previous examples already open, you will have to kill that process in order to run this one, as both of them use the same port.

To see the unit tests working, just execute the following:

```
node_modules/karma/bin/karma start
```

You should see a summary of five unit tests running in the terminal, and a continuous running process monitoring your project:

```
INFO [karma]: Karma v0.12.21 server started at
http://localhost:9876/
INFO [launcher]: Starting browser Chrome
INFO [Chrome 37.0.2062 (Mac OS X 10.9.5)]: Connected on socket
goMqmrnZkxyz9nlpQHem with id 16699326Chrome 37.0.2062 (Mac OS X 10.9.5):
Executed 5 of 5 SUCCESS
(0.018 secs / 0.013 secs)
```

We will explain how to write unit tests for the project later in this chapter. For a quick peek at what tests are running, look at `spec/viz_spec.js`.

If you change any of the methods in this file, you will notice that the test runner will detect that a change has been made in the code and re-execute the tests! This provides a fantastic feedback loop to the developer as you continue to enhance your work.

Exploring the code directory

In this section, we will cover each file in detail and explain its importance in the overall package:

- `index.html`: This file is the starting point of the visualization and will launch automatically when you point your browser to `http://localhost:8080`. You will notice that the file contains many of the points already covered in the book in terms of loading up the proper assets. As we walk through the `index.html` file, we will identify the other directories and files used in the project.

- `main.css`: The `main.css` file is used to apply specific CSS styling to your visualization:

  ```html
  <link rel="stylesheet" type="text/css" href="main.css">
  ```

- `vendor`: This directory contains all the external libraries that we need to use in the visualization and is loaded at the bottom of the `index.html` file:

  ```html
  <script src="vendor/d3.min.js"></script>
  <script src="vendor/topojson.v1.min.js"></script>
  ```

- We like to keep these to a minimum so that we have as few dependencies on the outside world as possible. In this case, we are only using the core D3 library and TopoJSON to help us with the GeoJSON encoding.

- `scripts`: This is another directory; there are some new additions to the files we are loading in order to create the visualization:

  ```html
  <!-- A base function for setting up the SVG and container -->
  <script src="scripts/base.js"></script>

  <!-- The main visualization code -->
  <script src="scripts/viz.js"></script>
  ```

- The `base.js` script contains some common D3 patterns that are reused in many examples (such as containing the visualization in a chart area <g> with a predefined margin object, common methods to calculate height and width based on this margin object, and a handy utility to find the existing container and binding data). The `base.js` script is also an excellent location to keep the reusable code.
- The `viz.js` script is an example that leverages many of the concepts in *Towards Reusable Charts* with some inheritance gained from `base.js`. The `viz.js` script is the workhorse of the project and where most of the visualization code will reside.

- `factories`: This too is a directory. In order to show our work in the browser, we need a script to generate some data, select the element in the DOM, and initiate the visualization call. These scripts are organized in the `factories` directory. An example of this can be viewed in the `viz_factory.js` file:

```
<!-- The script acts as a proxy to call the visualization
  and draw it with sample data -->
<script src="factories/viz_factory.js"></script>
```

- `spec`: The tests you write to validate the methods in the visualization code go here. A detailed example will be provided later in this chapter.

Other administrative files

Two additional files that assist with the operation of the Bootstrap project are as follows; these files rarely require any modification:

- `karma.conf.js`: This is used to set up the unit test runs
- `package.json`: This describes which npm packages to install

Writing testable code

There are dozens of factors to consider when creating visualizations. Every design will have its own set of unique requirements and configuration capabilities to consider. If you build on the reusable pattern outlined by Mike Bostock, you will have a great framework to start with.

When working with data visualizations, we will have some form of data manipulation or logic that must be applied to incoming data. There are two notable best practices we can leverage to test and validate these operations. They are explained in the following sections.

Keeping methods/functions small

Small functions mean low cyclomatic complexity. This means there are fewer logic branches in each function and, therefore, fewer things to test. If we test each simple function thoroughly and independently, then there will be fewer chances of things going wrong when we compose them together into larger complex computations. A good guideline is to try and keep methods at around 10 lines of code.

Preventing side effects

This basically means that each small function should not save some state outside itself. Try to limit the use of global variables as much as possible and think of each function as the following process:

1. Data arrives.
2. Perform some operations on the data.
3. Return results.

This way we can easily test each function independently, without worrying about the effect it has on the global state of the program.

An example with viz.js

To see this in practice, let's take a look at the `scripts/viz.js` program as a template for creating testable code for the data manipulation functions in the visualization. For this example, we will create a set of simple bars that are based on the profit of an arbitrary dataset. We are given the sales and cost in the data; however, we need to determine the profit for the visualization by subtracting the sales from the cost. In this contrived example, we need a few small helper functions, which are as follows:

- A function to take the original dataset and return a new dataset with the profit calculated
- A function to retrieve an array of unique categories to apply to an ordinal scale
- A function to determine the maximum profit value in order to build the upper bound of our input domain

If we create these functions with the best practices outlined earlier and expose them externally, we can test them in isolation and independently.

Let's take a tour of the script to see how it all works together:

```
if (d3.charts === null || typeof(d3.charts) !== 'object')
{ d3.charts = {}; }
```

Here, we will define the namespace for the chart. In this example, our chart can be instantiated with d3.charts.viz. If the d3 object with the charts property does not exist, or if it is not of the type object, create it, using classical functional inheritance to leverage common patterns from a base function:

```
d3.charts.viz = function () {
    // Functional inheritance of common areas
    var my = d3.ext.base();
```

A handy function (see base.js) to quickly assign getters/setters to the closure following the pattern in *Towards Reusable Charts* is as follows:

```
    // Define getter/setter style accessors..
    // defaults assigned
    my.accessor('example', true);
```

We use the svg variable at this level of scope to maintain state when quickly appending selectors. The void 0 is a safer way to initialize the variable as undefined:

```
    // Data for Global Scope
    var svg = void 0,
        chart = void 0;
```

Define the D3 instance functions that will be used throughout the visualization:

```
    // Declare D3 functions, also in instance scope
    var x = d3.scale.linear(),
        y = d3.scale.ordinal();
```

The following function represents the main interface to the outside world. There is also a set of setup functions commonly seen in D3 visualizations. The SVG container is set up in a way that can easily look for existing SVG containers in the selector and rebind the data. This makes it much easier to redraw when making subsequent calls with new data:

```
    my.draw = function(selection) {
      selection.each(function(data) {
        // code in base/scripts.js
        // resuable way of dealing with margins
        svg = my.setupSVG(this);
        chart = my.setupChart(svg);

        // Create the visualization
        my.chart(data);
      });
    };

    // main method for drawing the viz
```

```
my.chart = function(data) {
  var chartData = my.profit(data);

  x.domain([0, my.profitMax(chartData)])
      .range([0,my.w()]);
  y.domain(my.categories(chartData))
      .rangeRoundBands([0, my.h()], 0.2);

  var boxes = chart.selectAll('.box').data(chartData);

  // Enter
  boxes.enter().append('rect')
      .attr('class', 'box')
      .attr('fill', 'steelblue');

  // Update
  boxes.transition().duration(1000)
      .attr('x', 0)
      .attr('y', function(d) { return y(d.category) })
      .attr('width', function(d) {  return x(d.profit) })
      .attr('height', y.rangeBand())

  // Exit
  boxes.exit().remove();
};
```

Notice that the `chart` function relies on several helper functions (shown in the following lines of code) to work with the data. It is also written in such a way that we can take advantage of the enter/update/exit pattern:

```
// Example function to create profit.
my.profit = function(data) {
  return data.map(function(d) {
    d.profit = parseFloat(d.sales) - parseFloat(d.cost);
    return d;
  });
};
```

This function is used to create a new data structure that has profit assigned. Note that it takes one data array in as a parameter and returns a newly constructed array with the profit attribute added. This function is now exposed externally with `viz().profit(data)` and can be easily tested. It does not change any of the outside global variables. It is just data in and new data out:

```
my.categories = function(data) {
    return data.map(function(d) {
      return d.category;
    });
};
```

This is the exact same pattern as `my.profit(data)`. We will take the data structure in as input and return a new data structure, that is, an array of all the categories. In the preceding lines of code, you saw that this is leveraged to create the input domain.

```
my.profitMax = function(data) {
    return d3.max(data, function(d) { return d.profit; });
};
```

Once again, a simple function to take data in, compute the max, and return that maximum value. It is very easy to test and verify with `d3.charts.viz().profitMax(data)`?

```
    return my;
};
```

Unit testing

Now that we have a code base written in a testable way, let's automate those tests so that we do not have to perform them manually and can continue to code and refactor with ease.

If you look at the `spec/viz_spec.js` file, you will note some common patterns when unit testing. The following code is written with a JavaScript unit-testing framework called Jasmine and leverages Karma to execute the tests. You can learn more about the Jasmine syntax, assertions, and other features at `http://jasmine.github.io/1.3/introduction.html`.

The Bootstrap project has everything you need to start testing quickly.

The first step is to start our Karma test runner with this line of code:

```
node_modules/karma/bin/karma start
```

This runner will watch every edit of the `viz.js` file or the `viz_spec.js` file. If any changes are detected, it will automatically rerun every test suite and provide the output on the console. If all the tests pass, then the output will be all green. If something fails, you will receive a red warning message:

```
'use strict';

describe('Visualization: Stacked', function () {
  var viz;

  var data = [
    {"category": "gold",  "cost": "10",  "sales": "60"},
    {"category": "white", "cost": "20",  "sales": "30"},
    {"category": "black", "cost": "100", "sales": "140"}
  ];
```

Create some test data to test your D3 data manipulation functions. The preceding `describe` syntax defines the test harness you are about to execute:

```
beforeEach(function() {
  viz = d3.charts.viz()
    .height(600)
    .width(900)
    .margin({top: 10, right: 10, bottom: 10, left: 10});
});
```

Before every test run, create a new instance of the D3 visualization with some default setters:

```
it ('sets the profit', function() {
  var profits = viz.profit(data);
  expect(profits.length).toBe(3);
  expect(profits[0].profit).toBe(50)
});
```

This is our first test case! In this test, we asserted that we are getting a new array from our test data, but with an additional profit attribute. Remember that we created the function to have no side effects and to be a small unit of work. We will reap the fruits of our labor with this easy-to-test method. Just as we did earlier, we will test the list of categories now:

```
it ('returns a list of all categories', function() {
  var categories = viz.categories(data);
  expect(categories.length).toBe(3);
  expect(categories).toEqual([ 'gold', 'white', 'black' ]);
});
```

Calculate the maximum profit, as follows:

```
it ('calculates the profit max', function() {
  var profits = viz.profit(data);
  expect(viz.profitMax(profits)).toEqual(50);
});
```

The following are additional example tests to validate that the height/width, bearing in mind the margins, is working properly from our base.js function:

```
it ('calculates the height of the chart box', function() {
  expect(viz.h()).toBe(580);
  viz.height(700); // change the height
  viz.margin({top: 20, right: 10, bottom: 10, left: 10})
  expect(viz.h()).toBe(670);
});

it ('calculates the width of the chart box', function() {
  expect(viz.w()).toBe(880);
  viz.height(700); // change the height
  viz.margin({top: 10, right: 10, bottom: 10, left: 20})
  expect(viz.w()).toBe(870);
});
```

As an experiment, try adding new test cases or editing the existing one. Watch the test runner report different results.

Creating resilient visualization code

We want to make sure that our visualization can react to changing data, with minimal effort from the program that calls our code. One way to test different permutations of data and ensure that the visualization reacts accordingly is to randomly create example data, call the visualization code a number of times, and witness the result. These operations are handled in the factories directory. Let's take a look at the viz_factory.js file as an example:

```
(function() {
    var viz = d3.charts.viz();
```

Create a variable to store our function with `getters` and `setters` as closures. In this example, we will use an anonymous function as a wrapper to execute the code. This prevents conflicts with other JavaScript code and ensures that our visualization will work properly in a protected context:

```
var rand = function() {
  return Math.floor((Math.random() * 10) + 1)
};
```

A simple helper function that generates a random number between 1 and 10 is as follows:

```
var data = function() {
  return [1,2,3].map(function(d,i) {
    var cost = rand();
    var sales = rand();

    return {
      category: 'category-'+i,
      cost: cost,
      sales: cost + sales
    };
  });
};
```

Generate a fake dataset based on random numbers:

```
d3.select("#chart").datum(data()).call(viz.draw);
```

Draw the visualization for the first time using these lines of code:

```
var id = setInterval(function() {
  var d = data();
  console.log('data:', d);
  d3.select("#chart").datum(d).call(viz.draw);
}, 2000);
setTimeout(function() {
clearInterval(id);
}, 10000);
```

Set a timer for 10 seconds and bind new data to the visualization on iteration. The expected behavior is that the visualization will redraw itself on each call. Notice how simple it is to pass new data to the visualization. It is a simple selector with a new dataset. We have constructed the reusable visualization code in such a way that it knows how to react appropriately.

To see the results in action, simply launch `http-server`, as follows:

```
node_modules/http-server/bin/http-server
```

Now, visit `http://localhost:8080`.

Adding a new test case

What happens if we change the number of datasets in the array? To test this, let's add a new helper function (called `set()`) to randomly generate a new set of data with a random number of elements between 1 and 10:

```
var set = function() {
  var k = rand();
  var d = [];
  for (var i = 1; i < k; i++) {
    d.push[i];
  };
  return d;
};
```

Modify the `data` function slightly. We will print to the console to validate that it is working properly:

```
var data = function() {
  var d = set();
  console.log('d', d);
  return d.map(function(d,i) {
    var cost = rand();
    var sales = rand();

    return {
      category: 'category-'+i,
      cost: cost,
      sales: cost + sales
    };
  });
};
```

Now, if we look at `http://localhost:8080` again, we can see that the visualization is working properly even with a random amount of data.

Summary

In this chapter, we described the techniques to help test your D3 code base and to keep it healthy over the lifespan of your project. We also went step by step through a Bootstrap project to help you get started with these examples, and we took a look at a methodology for structuring your work.

Our recommendations are based on many years of experience and many projects delivered using D3. We strongly recommend that you follow good software patterns and focus on tests; this will allow you to perfect your craft. Quality is in your hands now.

8

Drawing with Canvas and D3

So far you have used D3 to render your visualizations with mostly SVG, and sometimes HTML, elements. In this section, you will learn how to use HTML5 Canvas to draw and animate your visualizations. Canvas can be used as an alternative to SVG, especially if you want to render more elements on screen. You will get an overview of what Canvas is and how it compares with SVG. You will learn how to draw and animate with Canvas and how you can use D3 with it.

After covering the foundations, we will visualize flight paths first with SVG and then with Canvas to contrast and compare the two rendering approaches hands on. First and foremost, this will give you a practical understanding of how Canvas works as an alternative to SVG. Secondly, it will showcase how Canvas can solve problems you might have when animating thousands of points at once with SVG, as browsers are significantly faster in drawing a single picture of thousands of elements than in building, storing, and maintaining a tree of thousands of elements in memory.

We will cover the following topics in this chapter:

- Overview of Canvas and its tools: the Canvas context
- How to use the tools to draw with Canvas
- How to animate a drawing with Canvas
- How to apply the D3 life cycle to individual parts of the Canvas drawing

Introducing Canvas

Before you start to draw with Canvas, let's have a brief look at its concept – the mental model that will help you approach, plan, and write your applications. Canvas in its material form is a single HTML5 element. It is literally a blank canvas that you can draw on. For the actual drawing, you use the **Canvas context** – the Canvas API. The context can be thought of as your toolbox that can be manipulated with JavaScript.

You can compare the Canvas element with the root SVG element, as both contain all parts of the drawing. However, the key difference is that SVG (like HTML) operates in **retained mode**. The browser retains a list of all objects drawn onto the SVG (or HTML) canvas within the **Document Object Model (DOM)** – the scene-graph of your web application. This makes your drawing almost material. You produce a list of objects, change styles and properties through code, and you can refer to these elements any time you desire. You can change their position, move them up or down the DOM and – very important for interaction – you can attach and remove event listeners to them easily.

Canvas, in contrast, operates in **immediate mode**. Anything you draw using Canvas occurs at once and remains on the canvas as an image. Images in Canvas are bitmaps, digital images composed of a matrix or grid of pixels. When you draw with Canvas you prepare the properties of each pixel (or rather specified regions of pixels) with your tools and then draw them on the canvas. If you want to change the color of one, a few, or all pixels on your image, you remove the whole image and produce a new image. Unlike SVG, you can't go back to the pixel you want to change, as it is not represented in memory in the form of a document tree or the like, but *burned* just once onto the screen. But fear not, you still have the Canvas context that represents the state of your tools, which indirectly represents the drawing itself.

You can think of Canvas as a painting and SVG or HTML as a Lego structure. The former is static in its representation. If you paint a man standing on a bridge screaming, you can't just turn his head around. You would have to draw a second painting to express this precisely. If you built the same scene with Lego, you could grab the head and turn it around, like so:

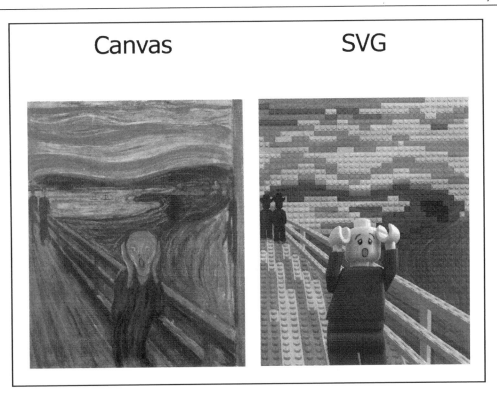

A dramatization of the immediate Canvas and the retained SVG

This might sound cumbersome, considering the potential work that has to go into animating with Canvas. Not just the mental strain of having to paint so many pictures, but the computational powers required to redraw everything in quick succession. But, as you will see in the coming sections, there are simple patterns that make Canvas animated and interactive.

Drawing with Canvas

Before we come back to a more thorough comparison of SVG and Canvas and see concrete scenarios of when to use what, let's learn to draw with Canvas. We will start with a very simple example to understand the three main steps involved when drawing with Canvas. Then you will draw a set of shapes to get used to its toolbox.

As a side note, when working along and viewing the code examples, I highly recommend you use a recent Chrome browser. All code is tested across modern browsers but has been written with Chrome in mind, which therefore will be the safest browser to work with.

The three drawing steps of every Canvas visual

We can deconstruct a Canvas drawing into three simple steps:

1. **Create** the canvas and its context.
2. **Configure** the context.
3. **Render** the resulting bitmap.

To mount the canvas within your DOM you create a `<canvas>` element in HTML:

```
<canvas id="main-canvas" width = "600" height="400"></canvas>
```

It will look empty, as expected:

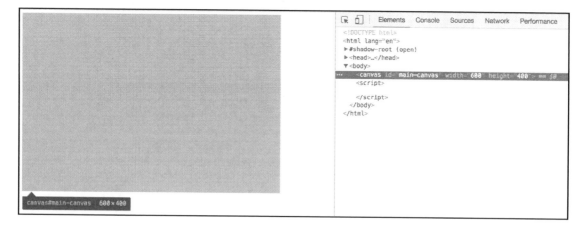

An empty Canvas element

This will be all the DOM you will see of your canvas. All other operations will happen via the Canvas context in JavaScript.

If you wanted to draw a rectangle in, say, `royalblue`, you would move onto JavaScript without looking back to the HTML and write:

```
var canvas = d3.select('#main-canvas').node();
var context = canvas.getContext('2d');

context.fillStyle = 'royalblue';
context.fillRect(50, 50, 200, 100);
```

You can find all code to this chapter at `https://github.com/larsvers/Learning-D3.js-4-Mapping`

Let's go through our first steps one by one:

1. First, you reference the canvas in a variable. We'll use `d3.select()` to do so. As you will need a reference to the canvas element itself, not a selection, you should use D3's `selection.node()` method to grab the element itself. The next line references the drawing context to this specific canvas element. The context includes all the tools you can use to draw. You can `console.log('context')` to have a look at the context object:

```
▼ CanvasRenderingContext2D {canvas: canvas#main-canvas, globalAlpha: 1, globalCompositeOperation: "source-over", filter: "none", imageSmoothingEnabled: true…}
  ▶ canvas: canvas#main-canvas
    fillStyle: "#008080"
    filter: "none"
    font: "10px sans-serif"
    globalAlpha: 1
    globalCompositeOperation: "source-over"
    imageSmoothingEnabled: true
    imageSmoothingQuality: "low"
    lineCap: "butt"
    lineDashOffset: 0
    lineJoin: "miter"
    lineWidth: 10
    miterLimit: 10
    shadowBlur: 0
    shadowColor: "rgba(0, 0, 0, 0)"
    shadowOffsetX: 0
    shadowOffsetY: 0
    strokeStyle: "#a52a2a"
    textAlign: "start"
    textBaseline: "alphabetic"
  ▶ __proto__: CanvasRenderingContext2D
```

The context object showing all properties

The context is called `CanvasRenderingContext2D` internally, but we will refer to it just as `context`. It holds all the properties you can manipulate to draw your visual. If you feel inclined you can also expand the `__proto__` object, which will show all methods available to you. We'll explain the key properties and methods as we go without diving into each individually. The important point of the context object is to understand that there's an object helping you to build your drawing. It stays at your side all along allowing you to use its methods and change its properties.

 A great place to learn more about the context API, its properties, and methods is the documentation on the Mozilla Developer Network at `https://developer.mozilla.org/en-US/docs/Web/API/CanvasRenderingContext2D`.

At this point, you have the canvas to draw on and the drawing tools, but you still haven't drawn anything.

2. In the second step you prepare the drawing. You configure the context to produce the desired drawing. The example is purposefully simple in that the only configuration is to set the fill of our yet non-existent object to `royalblue`. Note that `context.fillStyle` is a property, not a method, of the Canvas context. It's like you are a painter telling your brush box what color you want to use for the object you paint next.

3. This third step produces the following image. `context.fillRect()` takes four arguments: the *x* and the *y* position of the rectangle's starting point as well as the `width` and the `height`. Canvas – like SVG – uses a Cartesian co-ordinate system with the origin 0, 0 at the top-left corner increasing to the right and to the bottom. All values are given in pixels:

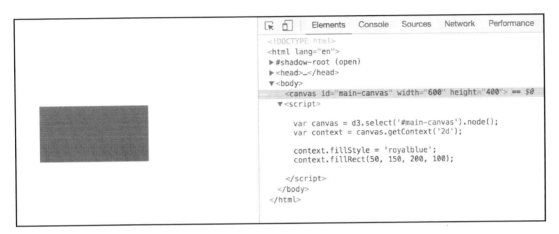

A very royal blue Canvas rectangle

This rectangle is not present in the DOM. You can see its configuration in JavaSript and the canvas its drawn to in the DOM, but there's no `<rect>` element or the like we could refer to. Again, don't grow worry lines; we will get clever about how to re-address it in the next two chapters.

View this step in the browser: `https://larsvers.github.io/learning-d3-mapping-8-1`. Code example `08_01.html`.

At the conclusion of each step you will find two links in an info box close to the the relevant image. The first link brings you to a working implementation of this step that you can view in the browser. The second *code example* link brings you to the full code. If you're reading the print version, you can find all code examples at `https://github.com/larsvers/Learning-D3.js-4-Mapping` in their relevant chapter.

You have seen the basic steps to follow when producing pretty much any drawing with Canvas. These key conceptual steps will help you to approach any Canvas drawing. Now let's draw more.

Drawing various shapes with Canvas

Let's add some other basic geometric shapes or **graphical primitives** to our canvas. As they are the building blocks of all the visuals you draw, some exercise will do us good. Here's what we will draw:

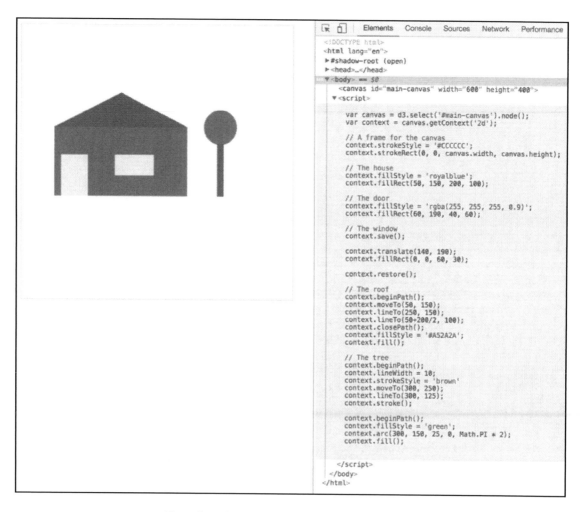

A house and a tree. Or three rectangles under a triangle next to a path and a circle.

View this step in the browser: https://larsvers.github.io/learning-d3-mapping-8-2. Code example 08_02.html.

You can see the code to the right in the JavaScript console, and before we step through it, let's note some general observations. First, every line starts with context. The Canvas context is really where our drawing comes to life. Second, Canvas code is written in a procedural style. This can be a benefit for beginners, as it is linear. No callbacks, no nested element structure, just a straight line of execution. This linearity will also extend to time, once you start animating the canvas. You write the first frame first, then you change the scene, then you write the second frame. Flip-book simple. Let's step through the code and see how to create these elements in detail. The first thing I suggest is giving the canvas a border. As the canvas element is an HTML element, you can style it with CSS, but we use JavaScript here to show off two properties of the canvas itself: width and height:

```
context.strokeStyle = '#CCCCCC';
context.strokeRect(0, 0, canvas.width, canvas.height);
```

The width and height are the only properties the canvas element has. We use them here to read the values of the element, however, they are readable and writable. This is nice, as you can change the canvas size programmatically when you want to resize your canvas during animation for example. Next, we build our flat-roofed blue house:

```
context.fillStyle = 'royalblue';
context.fillRect(50, 150, 200, 100);
```

Not much to see here, we've done that previously. The door won't make you sweat either, as it's the same as the house with a different color:

```
context.fillStyle = 'rgba(255, 255, 255, 0.9)';
context.fillRect(60, 190, 40, 60);
```

However, we use a different method to describe the color. You can use all CSS color concepts like named color values and hex color values, as well as the rgb(), rgba(), hsl() and hsla() color methods. The window is placed a little differently with context.translate():

```
context.save();
context.translate(140, 190);
context.fillRect(0, 0, 60, 30);
context.restore();
```

In this case, we don't move the rectangle, we move the entire coordinate system! The `translate()` method takes two arguments: the x and the y position you want to move the coordinate system by. You know this concept already from the use of `transform`, `translate(x,y)` which is often used to move `svg:g` elements in D3 and create their own coordinate systems. However, when applied to an `svg:g` element the transformed coordinate system applies to all objects nested within the g element. As said above, the g element, as well as its children, is retained as a scene-graph representation in the DOM, including its coordinate system. In Canvas, we can't move this information off to a representation of our drawing – there is no such thing. It's up to you to make sure only elements you want to manifest on a different coordinate system will do so. Remember above when we talked about the procedural style of writing Canvas code? This is exactly what we have to keep in mind here. When we change something in the `context` it will persist through our code until we change it again. To change the coordinate system back we could alternatively move it to our desired position and move it back afterwards like:

```
context.translate(140, 190);
context.fillRect(0, 0, 60, 30);
context.translate(-140, -190);
```

But we rather use the generally applicable `context.save()` and `context.restore()` methods. The `context.save()` saves the state at this point of the code and pushes it onto a **stack**, and `context.restore()` pops the last saved state off the stack and restores the previous state of the context. If you haven't come across stacks so far, here's an image explaining what it does:

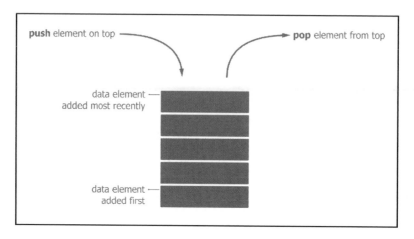

The stacked tower of data.

In short, a stack is a datatype like an array or an object. However, a stack is limited to two operations: adding elements on top of the stack (push) and removing elements from the top of the stack (pop). It's like a brick tower. This care-taking of our application's state is a defining aspect of Canvas and a key difference to SVG.

Next, we give the house a triangular roof. There's no `triangle()` function in Canvas, so you draw a path:

```
context.beginPath();
context.moveTo(50, 150);
context.lineTo(250, 150);
context.lineTo(50+200/2, 100); // you can use calculations as inputs!
context.closePath();
context.fillStyle = '#A52A2A';
context.fill();
```

Finally, we draw the tree. A tree has a brown stem, which you implement as a straight path, and a green treetop, which you draw as a green circle:

```
context.beginPath();
context.lineWidth = 10;
context.strokeStyle = 'brown'
context.moveTo(300, 250);
context.lineTo(300, 200);
context.stroke();

context.beginPath();
context.fillStyle = 'green';
context.arc(300, 175, 25, 0, Math.PI * 2);
context.fill();
```

There are two things to note here. First, all path code blocks are bracketed by `beginPath()` and either `stroke()` (the stem) or `fill()` (the roof and treetop):

```
context.beginPath();
// configure your path here
context.stroke();

context.beginPath();
// configure your path here
context.fill();
```

`beginPath()` signifies the intent to draw a new path and removes all current path (or sub-path) implementations. `stroke()` and `fill()` signify the end of the path and will produce the path on the screen. `fill()` will fill the path body with the set `fillStyle` color, and `stroke()` will only draw the path contour in with the set `strokeStyle()` method. Whenever you draw a path, you will need these start and end methods. In fact, whenever you draw anything you will need them. `fillRect()` or `strokeRect()`, as used previously, are just wrappers for beginning a path, drawing a path, and filling or stroking a path. You might have noticed that we only drew two sides of the triangular roof and then used `closePath()` which connects the current endpoint of the path with the starting point. The `fill()` method will also close the path for you, but making this explicit is more thorough, more performant and a service to the reader of your code (including yourself). The second thing to note is that even a circle is a path. In fact, the only primitive shape beyond a path offered by the Canvas API is the rectangle. SVG facilitates the use of `<rect>`, `<circle>`, `<ellipse>`, `<line>`, `<polyline>`, `<polygon>`, and `<path>`, while Canvas only offers paths and rectangles. However, drawing shapes with paths quickly becomes routine. While there is no pre-defined circle, there's the `arc()` and `arcTo()` methods, which pretty much do the circle drawing for you. You just need to add color to it and wrap it into the path start and end methods. `arc()` takes five arguments, the x and the y position, the *radius*, the *start* and the *end angle* of our arc. Both angles are being measured in radians.

A radian? One **radian** equals 57.3 degrees. Radians are an alternative unit of measurement for angles. They are beloved by mathematicians as they make a lot of sense in geometric calculations. To get a radian, you take the radius of a circle and wrap it around that circle – if you can imagine that the radius line is bendable:

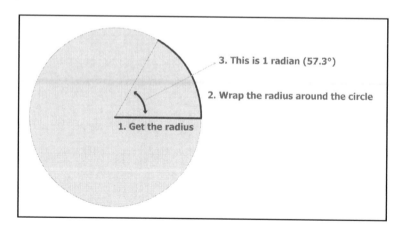

How to get a radian

Their mathematical advantage is that they can be derived directly from the radius of a circle. The further beauty is that half a circle (as in 180 degrees) is exactly one *PI* radians. Hence, a full circle equals *2 * PI* radians.

Degrees probably make more sense to you. That's fine. They also make more sense if you want to move objects around on the screen. You can easily convert between radians and degrees by using the following formula: *(PI / 180) * degrees*. PI is half a circle in radians and 180 is half a circle in degrees. By dividing one by the other, you express one degree in radians, which equals 0.0175. Multiply any degree number you desire with 0.0175 and use the result as radians.

OK! We've drawn a landscape with a house – that's great. There is certainly more to Canvas, but by following these simple steps you have learned a lot. You have learned about the concept of drawing with Canvas and what it means to write your code procedurally. You have seen how to draw individual shapes with Canvas, how you can move individual objects around with a translate transformation, and how the atomic unit of each Canvas shape is the path. Now, let's step it up and animate our landscape the Canvas way before we do it the D3 way.

Animating the Canvas

One of Canvas's key advantages is animation. While the browser must work hard to re-calculate and re-render many elements retained in a DOM, it is relatively unstressed re-drawing a bitmapped image. In the following section, you will learn how to animate with Canvas. Let's first look at how you do it in a pure, vanilla Canvas way. After that, let's see if we can use D3's transition and life cycle Enter-Update-Exit pattern to help us animate. Both ways will be immensely helpful when building visualizations with D3 and Canvas as you will be able to choose the right technique for your own ideas or complement the two.

Animating the Canvas way

Let's go back to our house and test its roof with rain:

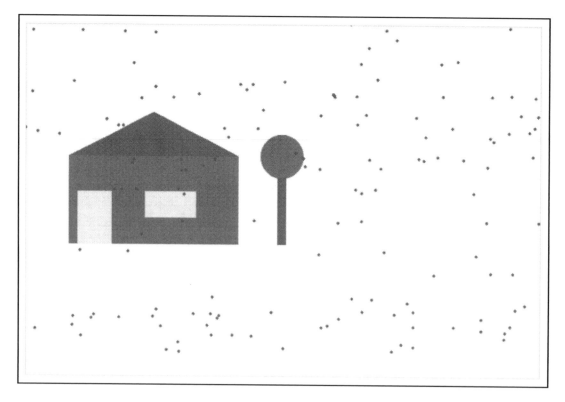

It's really raining.

 View this step in the browser: https://larsvers.github.io/learning-d3-mapping-8-3. Code example 08_03.html.

It's hard to see in a static image, but the blue dots are in fact moving down when viewed in the browser. They are also moving at different speeds, which makes the rain look a little more realistic.

Getting a general overview

On the abstracted top level our code looks as follows:

```
var canvas = d3.select('#main-canvas').node();  // set up
var context = canvas.getContext('2d');

var rain = { }                                   // produce data
d3.interval(function() {
    update();                                    // update/process the data
    animate();                                   // re-draw the canvas
}, 10);
```

After setting up the canvas, you will produce some data – the raindrops. Then you will enter a loop within which you will update the data for the next scene and then draw it. In our case, update() changes the raindrops' positions and animate() will clear the current image and draw a new image with the updated raindrop positions.

This loop (or at least a very similar incarnation) is called the **game loop**, as it is used in game programming with Canvas. You process the gamer's input, update the game data accordingly, and draw the new scene. We will get used to this pattern quickly. Now, let's look at the details.

Preparing the rain data

The elements you're dealing with are raindrops. Before we update or animate a single raindrop, we produce them. We're building out a so called *object literal module* called rain (it's an *object literal*) that knows how to produce raindrops and that keeps the individual drops save in an array called items. It will look like so:

```
var rain = {
    items: [],
    maxDrops: 200,
    getDrop: function() {
      var obj = {};
      obj.xStart = Math.floor(Math.random() * canvas.width);
      obj.yStart = Math.floor(Math.random() * -canvas.height);
      obj.x = null;
      obj.y = null;
      obj.speed = Math.round(Math.random() * 2) + 5;

      return obj;
    },
    updateDrop: // see below
    }
```

The `rain` object consists of this as yet empty array `items` that will hold all the raindrop objects we produce and a variable called `maxDrops`, confining the number of raindrops (the length of `items`) to 200 in this case. This can be considered light rain. Crank this up to a higher number if you want to drown the tree or test the app's performance. As we like the tree and shall test performance in an example to come, 200 will do for now.

Two functions will help to produce and update the drops. `getDrop()` assigns start positions out of sight above the canvas, as well as empty x and y positions which will be filled on update. You also define the speed of the drop, which can take on values between five and seven. The speed will be the number of pixels the raindrop will move forward on each update. A low number will produce slow rain and a higher number will produce fast rain.

The `updateDrop()` function can be called in case we, well, want to update a drop's position. Let's do this now.

Updating each drop

The site loads and things will kick off with the `d3.interval` function, which calls all functions it embraces every 10 milliseconds. First, it will call `update()` which returns an array of objects. Each object is a drop most notably characterized by an arbitrary x and y position. This is how it looks:

```
function update() {
  if (!rain.items.length) {
    d3.range(rain.maxDrops).forEach(function(el) {
      var drop = rain.getDrop(el);
      rain.updateDrop(drop);
      rain.items.push(drop);
    });
  } else {
    rain.items.forEach(function(el) {
      rain.updateDrop(el);
    });
  }
}
```

The first time `update()` is called it produces a drop, updates its position, and pushes it into the rain items array. Any other time, it just updates the drop's position. We use `d3.range` as a convenient method for this loop. It takes an integer as input and returns an array of integers starting at 0, and the length of the number you pass in. Here it helps create as many rain drops as we specified in `maxDrops`.

We then update the drop's position with the `updateDrop()` function we started to describe previously:

```
updateDrop: function(drop) {
    drop.x = drop.x === null ? drop.xStart : drop.x;
    drop.y = drop.y === null ? drop.yStart : drop.y + drop.speed;
    drop.y = drop.y > canvas.height ? drop.yStart : drop.y;
}
```

If the drop's x and y positions don't exist yet (if they are `null`) we assign the `xStart` or `yStart` values to it. If not, we leave the x position where it is as no drop will move to any side, and we move the y position downwards by speed. This will make the drop move down between five and seven pixels every 10 milliseconds. The last line recycles each drop. Once it has reached the final border of the bottom canvas, we just set its y value to the initial `yStart` value.

Drawing frame by frame

Back in our `d3.interval` loop, `update()` has run and we have the positions of all our raindrops. Next, we will deal with drawing them. If we had a DOM, we would interact with our omnipresent 200 SVG circles and ask them kindly to move down a little. But we produce a static image and we can only draw and not change. So, we draw. Like in a flip book we dispose of the old image and draw a new one. Let's repeat this. Each time we want to move something on the canvas we **remove the old image** and **draw a new image** with changed positions.

It's straightforward:

```
function animate() {
    context.clearRect(0, 0, canvas.width, canvas.height);
    drawScene();
    rain.items.forEach(function(el) {
        circle(context, el.x, el.y, 1.5, 'blue');
    });
}
```

`animate()` uses the context's own `clearRect()` function, which does what it says on the tin. You pass it the area you want to clear – in our case the entire canvas – and it will clear it. You can also fill a white rectangle or change the `canvas.width` and `canvas.height` values, but `clearRect()` is faster than the first and clearer than the second method.

Next, you run the drawScene() function, which draws our scene: the house and the tree. It's what you built in the previous section, just wrapped up in an aptly-named function.

Finally, we draw each drop to the canvas. What is circle() you ask? It's a helper function to build visual primitives – in our case a circle. It has been added at the top of the code:

```
function circle(ctx, x, y, r, color) {
  ctx.beginPath();
  ctx.fillStyle = color;
  ctx.arc(x, y, r, 0, 2 * Math.PI);
  ctx.fill();
}
```

The two main functions update() and animate() are being run repeatedly until the end of your browser tab's session; which could mean bad weather for some time.

Canvas and D3

D3 offers unmatched functionality for producing data visualizations on the web. You might be aware of this, reading this very book. One important part of what D3 offers is its model for how data-infused elements evolve on the screen. It has a certain way of thinking about the life cycle of each element.

In practice, you inject data into a yet non-existent DOM, and D3 creates new elements of your choice as per the data you inject, usually one element per data point. If you want to inject new data into the DOM you can do so and D3 identifies which elements have to be newly created, which elements are allowed to stay, and which elements should pack up and leave the screen. This way you can represent three distinct states of a common data-flow: **entering** data, **updating** data, and **exiting** data. You can then grab these selections, manipulate their visual properties as well as transition between them with D3's built-in interpolators, leveraged by d3.transition().

This plays well with the retained SVG elements that are manifested in the DOM. However, we have no DOM elements in the canvas and must, therefore, be a little clever about producing them. Let's see how we can follow D3's life cycle model as well as using D3's transitions to interpolate between these three states.

Getting an overview of our experiment

We will still let it rain over our little house and its tree, but now the rain will follow its natural course – the rain's life cycle, as it were. It will **Enter** in the form of a cloud, it will **Update** as the rain moving into a big puddle on the ground, and it will **Exit** turning the puddle into a lush patch of grass:

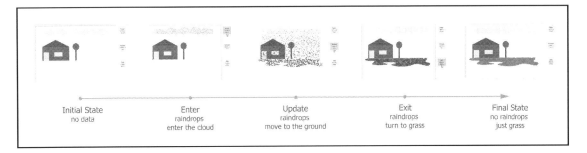

Initial State	Enter	Update	Exit	Final State
no data	raindrops enter the cloud	raindrops move to the ground	raindrops turn to grass	no raindrops just grass

Enter, Update and Exit the rain

View this step in the browser: `https://larsvers.github.io/learning-d3-mapping-8-4b`. **Code example** `08_04b.html`.

As you can see, there are buttons to the right allowing you to control the three state changes.

The structure of the code will be similar to the previous pure Canvas animation. Conceptually, you calculate the elements' (the raindrops') positions first and then draw. However, the way we achieve this interaction is entirely via D3. To lift the lid in advance, you will bind the data to virtual DOM elements. These DOM elements are 'virtual'. As Canvas has no DOM, you create a basic DOM structure in memory, with which we can use D3's selections, the data join, and consequently the Enter-Update-Exit API. Additionally, the app will have button interactions to change the elements' state according to the changed data. We have discussed the Canvas setup as well as data preparation already, so let's focus on the core novelty of this section, the databind and the draw!

The data

Having said that, we should have a brief look at the data we will produce with a function called `getRainData()`. It will give us 2,500 raindrops (heavy rain this time) that look a little different to our previous example:

```
              The first raindrop object
                  of the rain array


  ▼ 0: Object                    ▼ 0: Object
      currentIndex: 0                currentIndex: 0
      speed: 5                       radiusCloud: 1
      x: 465                         radiusGrass: 8
      xStart: 465                    radiusPuddle: 2
      y: -18                         xCloud: 252.961035374657
      yStart: -353                   xPuddle: 252.961035374657
                                     yCloud: 19.51464792726162
                                     yPuddle: 309.9218482689457


      Vanilla Canvas                 D3 and Canvas
```

A raindrop the Vanilla Canvas way versus a raindrop the D3-and-Canvas way

The key differences are that you don't need the speed for the D3 raindrop version, as we plan for D3's transition to implement the animation. Further, the **D3 and Canvas** raindrop has properties for a set of states included, while the **Vanilla Canvas** raindrop only has start and current positions.

Updating each drop

With the data in place, it's now time to make it move. In the pure Canvas example, you drew each point on the canvas, then calculated new points adding five pixels to the previous point's position, removed the old image, and drew the new one with the advanced drops. You transitioned the points yourself.

Employing D3's transition methods differs in that we won't calculate the new position, but D3 will do it for us. You will bind the data to selections, ask D3 to transition the values, and while it transitions you will redraw the canvas for as long as the transition runs. On a top level, you only need two functions to do this:

```
databind(data) {
  // Bind data to custom elements.
}
draw() {
  // Draw the elements on the canvas.
}
```

It's pretty straightforward.

Binding the data

However, D3 implements transitions on selections, and we don't have selections yet. A single D3 selection is an element with bound data. With D3 you select a DOM element, usually SVG, join data to it, and you have a selection with all its wondrous methods: the explicit `enter()` and `exit()` methods, the implicit `update()` method triggered by `data()`, as well as `transition()` and their helpers `duration()` and `delay()` that control the transition.

To create selections, you just create DOM-like elements, and the great thing is, you don't need the incarnated DOM to do so. You can create them in memory. Here's how:

```
var customBase = document.createElement('custom')
var custom = d3.select(customBase);
```

You can imagine `customBase` as a replacement of a root SVG element and `custom` to be a fully-fledged D3 selection. With your foundation in place you can go about the usual D3 business of binding data to your custom elements with the `databind()` function:

```
function databind(data) { }
```

First, we join the data passed into the `databind()` function:

```
var join = custom.selectAll('custom.drop')
    .data(data, function(d) { return d.currentIndex; });
```

 The key function passed in as the second argument to `data` isn't strictly necessary in this case, but is good practice as it makes the join unambiguous and can have performance benefits.

Now you create your selection states. The `enter` selection is first:

```
var enter = join
  .enter().append('custom')
    .attr('class', 'drop')
    .attr('cx', function(d) { return d.xCloud; })
    .attr('cy', function(d) { return d.yCloud; })
    .attr('r', function(d) { return d.radiusCloud; })
    .attr('fillStyle', 'rgba(0, 0, 255, 0')
  .transition().delay(function(d, i) { return i * 2; })
    .attr('fillStyle', 'rgba(0, 0, 255, 0.2');
```

There are two things of note about the two bottom lines setting the `fillStyle` attribute. When you work with SVG the last line would be:

```
.style('color', 'rgba(0, 0, 255, 0.2')
```

But with Canvas you use `.attr()`. Why? Your main interest here is to find a pain-free way to transfer some element-specific information. Here you want to transfer a color string from the `databind()` to the `draw()` function. You use the element simply as a vessel to transport your data over to where it is being rendered to the canvas.

That's a very important distinction: when working with SVG or HTML you can bind data to elements and draw or apply styles to the elements in one step. In Canvas, you need two steps. First, you bind the data then you draw the data. You can't style the elements while binding. They only exist in memory and Canvas can't be styled via CSS style properties, which is exactly what you access when using `.style()`.

Let's have a quick look at how the `customBase` element looks after we've created and appended the `enter` selection to it:

```
> customBase
< ▼<custom>
    <custom class="drop" cx="402.98612497357414" cy="52.67184913996267" r="1" fillstyle="rgba(0, 0, 255, 0.2"></custom>
    <custom class="drop" cx="348.67239491322" cy="24.617968846763837" r="1" fillstyle="rgba(0, 0, 255, 0.2"></custom>
    <custom class="drop" cx="538.2821069419892" cy="58.73954122604771" r="1" fillstyle="rgba(0, 0, 255, 0.2"></custom>
    <custom class="drop" cx="375.200334667349" cy="26.139568948071652" r="1" fillstyle="rgba(0, 0, 255, 0.2"></custom>
    <custom class="drop" cx="407.43256562543274" cy="50.25992840177555" r="1" fillstyle="rgba(0, 0, 255, 0.2"></custom>
    <custom class="drop" cx="302.0967106310143" cy="13.331625298065198" r="1" fillstyle="rgba(0, 0, 255, 0.2"></custom>
```

Our custom root element showing 30 of our raindrops in enter-state

Looks familiar in structure, doesn't it?

Next, you define the `update` selection, and finally the `exit` selection:

```
var update = join
  .transition()
    .duration(function() { return Math.random() * 1000 + 900; })
    .delay(function(d,i) { return (i / data.length) * dur; })
    .ease(d3.easeLinear)
    .attr('cx', function(d) { return d.xPuddle; })
    .attr('cy', function(d) { return d.yPuddle; })
    .attr('r', function(d) { return d.radiusPuddle; })
    .attr('fillStyle', '#0000ff');

var exit = join
  .exit().transition()
    .duration(dur)
    .delay(function(d,i) { return i ; })
    .attr('r', function(d) { return d.radiusGrass; })
    .attr('fillStyle', '#01A611');
```

That's all that goes into `databind()`.

Drawing the data

Now you need to write the `draw()` function to get the elements on screen. Let's just note here that nothing has happened yet. You haven't called `databind()` yet because you need to find a way to draw it to the canvas first. So, off we go.

The `draw()` function takes the context you want to draw on as an argument:

```
function draw(ctx) {
  ctx.clearRect(0, 0, canvas.width, canvas.height);

  drawRainScene();
  drawScene();

  var elements = custom.selectAll('custom.drop');
  elements.each(function(d, i) {
    var node = d3.select(this);
    ctx.save();
    ctx.beginPath();
    ctx.globalCompositeOperation = 'source-atop'
    ctx.fillStyle = node.attr('fillStyle');
    ctx.arc(node.attr('cx'), node.attr('cy'), node.attr('r'), 0, 2 *
    Math.PI);
    ctx.fill();
```

```
        ctx.restore();
    });
```

Then it does the following:

1. It clears the canvas.
2. It draws the background scene, including the house and tree, as well as a cloud and a puddle drawn in `drawRainScene()`.
3. It loops through each of our virtual elements to draw it according to the attributes we specified in `databind()`.

That's it! You can close the `draw()` function.

See the line `ctx.globalCompositeOperation = 'source-atop'`? The `globalCompositeOperation` allows us to fuse or blend-in shapes. It operates on a source shape, the shape we are about to draw, and a destination, the Canvas content *underneath* the source shape. You can apply a number of compositing effects, but we use `source-atop` here.

Check `https://developer.mozilla.org/en-US/docs/Web/API/CanvasRenderingContext2D/globalCompositeOperation` for all composite options.

As a result, the new shape is only drawn where it overlaps the existing canvas content. The shape will not be visible in canvas regions without any drawings. This is why we need all objects in `drawRainScene()`. They form the background to our raindrops which they can't escape. By the way, if you don't want to draw all complex shapes by hand, you can draw them with vector graphics software such as Illustrator, save them as SVG, and use apps such as the *SVG to HTML5 Canvas converter* at `http://www.professorcloud.com/svg-to-canvas/` to convert SVG paths into Canvas commands.

Running the app

So far, no raindrop has shown itself, but you have the background scene in place:

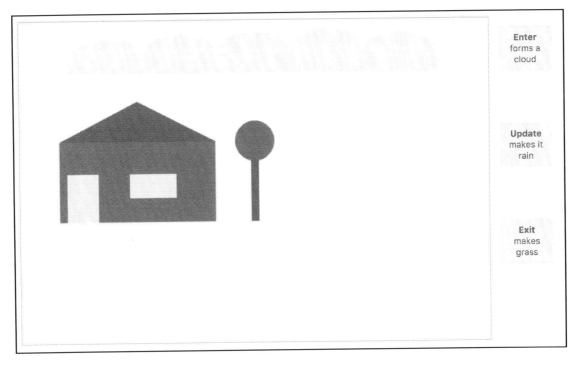

The initial scene

You have the means to animate the life cycle with the `databind()` and the `draw()` functions. You just call them in a sequence and wire this call-up with the buttons. Let's play this through for the **Enter** case. The cloud is empty and we want raindrops to transition into play from 0 to 0.2 opacity, that's how we specified it in the `databind()` function. We could just run:

```
databind(raindata);
draw(context);
```

This will join the data to the custom elements and, as all elements are joined with new data, draw the enter selection – once! But we need to display the transition, so we need to draw repeatedly while the transition is happening. You achieve this with a continuous loop:

```
databind(data);
var t = d3.timer(function(elapsed) {
  draw(context);
    if (elapsed > dur * 2) t.stop();
});
```

First, we bind the incoming data to our custom elements. Then we draw repeatedly. `d3.timer()` calls its callback repeatedly until you tell it to stop. The callback takes an argument we call `elapsed` here, which is the time in milliseconds the timer is running. The `draw()` function will be run many times drawing the background scene as well as each raindrop. At the same time a transition is running within `databind()`, changing each raindrop's position slightly. The `draw()` function will pick up these slight position changes as it loops through each raindrop every time it's called, drawing the raindrop at the very position the transition in `databind()` sets it to at this given moment. You can think of it as two processes happening at the same time: the transition in `databind()` delivering new raindrop positions and the repeated canvas drawing in `draw()` removing the previous canvas and drawing these new raindrop positions.

After the transition is done, we want to stop the timer. Work done. The transition in `databind()` runs for 2000 milliseconds, as we set it in the `dur` variable. We shall use `dur` now to clear up after us. We can stop any timer from within calling the timer's `.stop()`-method. To be safe we call `t.stop()` after we're passed double our duration `dur` (*4000* milliseconds) to cater for delayed transitions.

This is how a D3 transition works in Canvas. You call the drawing function more or less parallel to the binding function repeatedly Whatever style or position properties your D3 elements are set up to transition (*x, y, color, width, height,* for example.), they will be redrawn many times with small incremental changes for each draw.

Wiring it up to the buttons is a formality. Just wrap the `databind()` and `draw()` functions into a function (we shall call it `rainAnimation()`) that passes in the `raindata` when the enter or update button is pressed and an empty array when the exit button is pressed.

That's it!

The rain cloud will appear on the screen upon hitting the **Enter** button:

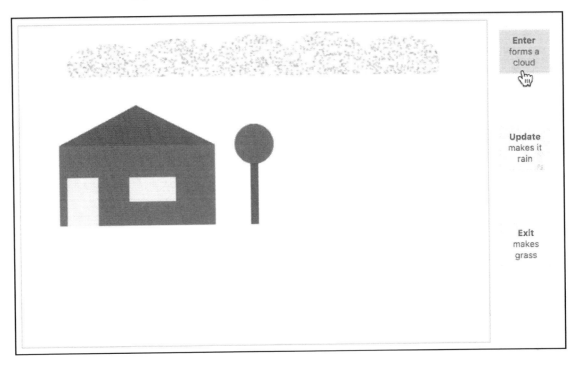

Enter rain into cloud

The **Update** button will update the rain's position from the cloud to a puddle:

Update rain to the ground

The **Exit** button will finally turn the rain into grass:

Exit the rain to become grass

 View this step in the browser: `https://larsvers.github.io/learning-d3-mapping-8-4a`. Code example `08_04a.html`.

A natural D3 life cycle demonstration!

Summary

You've come a long way. You've learned how to draw with Canvas, how to animate the canvas in a pure Canvas way, as well as how to use D3 transitions and the Enter-Update-Exit pattern with Canvas. While the Vanilla Canvas way is perfectly reasonable for a great many applications, D3 offers seasoned functionality for data visualization you don't have to abandon. It requires a shift in thinking when building your application, but it can pay out specifically for drawing and animating a large number of points. It will expand your toolbox in a valuable way, especially at times where abundant data might require element-heavy representations.

In the next chapter, we will review a map visualization in SVG and then build one in Canvas. By doing so, you will not only be able to apply the learnings from this chapter, but you will also learn more about the differences and similarities between the two approaches, how Canvas can help with performance bottlenecks, and how D3 can help with some heavy lifting.

Let's get to it!

9

Mapping with Canvas and D3

It's time to leave our house and tree. I know it's sad, but we'll move on to potentially more exciting things to build. You covered a lot of ground in the previous chapter. You learned how to draw with Canvas, how to animate with Canvas, and a pattern to combine the D3 life cycle with Canvas. As D3 is usually in cahoots with SVG, you also learned about a few key differences between SVG and Canvas. Understanding the advantages and limitations of either approach is key to making informed decisions about which mode of rendering to use. Here's what we will go through in this chapter:

- We'll start off with a summary of the key reasons for using either SVG or Canvas.
- We will then move on to review steps to build a flight path visualization with SVG, before building one with Canvas.
- Along the way, we will focus on measuring the performance to get a good understanding of how far we can go with either approach.

This will further contrast and compare the two approaches conceptually and technically. It will also allow us to demonstrate the main reason for choosing Canvas over SVG – animation of a great many points.

Choosing Canvas or SVG

You have already seen some benefits and some challenges to overcome when working with either of the two rendering methods. This section is supposed to summarize the most important differences. As such, it should give you a good understanding of what to use in which circumstance. Note, that I am juxtaposing SVG and Canvas rather than HTML and SVG with Canvas. It seems appropriate to focus on SVG as it is D3's main building block due to its visualization advantages. However, the same logic applies to the equally retained HTML.

Reasons to choose SVG

Let's first look at the SVG benefits:

- SVG is a vector-based graphics system. It allows resolution independent drawings you can scale without affecting quality.
- You can easily access elements in the DOM to move, change, or add interactivity.
- You can style with CSS.
- D3 works closely with the DOM, allowing for concise operations such as element selection and styling in a single pass and declarative animations with SVG.
- SVG is accessible to screen-readers and SEO bots out of the box. Canvas requires fallback text or a sub-DOM to provide some level of accessibility.

Reasons to choose Canvas

While SVG might be easier to handle, Canvas has advantages when it comes to showing and animating more elements:

- SVG allows you to draw roughly 10,000 elements and animate 1,000 or so elements. With Canvas you can animate around 10,000 points. Why? First of all, Canvas is lower level and has fewer abstraction layers to keep and manage in memory. Secondly, browsers (like most monitors) mostly support a frame rate of 60 frames per second, meaning the screen is updated 60 times per second. This leaves *1000 / 60 = 16.67* milliseconds to finish all necessary rendering and housekeeping activities. As human brains are fooled into perceiving fluid animation at a mere 16 frames per second, the maximum time for rendering a frame is *1000 / 16 = 62.5* milliseconds — but you should strive for a shorter time. For SVG these activities include DOM parsing, render tree production, layout and screen painting, to name the most important. The path between Canvas changes and image is shorter. The browser turns the context instructions into an array of pixel values before painting it to the canvas.
- If you need more elements to render or animate, accessing the alternative WebGL context is as easy as defining `canvas.getContext('webgl')`. WebGL allows you to animate 100k elements and more. While WebGL code is close to GPU programming and hence not for the faint-hearted, abstraction libraries like `Three.js`, `Pixi.js`, or `regl` make it more accessible.

Check out Peter Beshai's excellent tutorial on animating 100,000 points with WebGl and regl at `https://peterbeshai.com/beautifully-animate-points-with-webgl-and-regl.html`.

- Canvas is a **rasterized** graphics system. This just means the image consists of a *raster* (we could also say a *matrix*) of pixels. As a result, scaling can lead to blur, but in turn it's simple to download your canvas as an image. A further problem are high **Dots Per Inch (DPI)** or retina screens, that can make Canvas blur. You can use the following setup to support retina displays on Canvas:

```
var devicePixelRatio = window.devicePixelRatio || 1
var canvas = d3.select('body').append('canvas')
    .attr('width', width * devicePixelRatio)
    .attr('height', height * devicePixelRatio)
    .style('width', width + 'px')
    .style('height', height + 'px');
var context = canvas.getContext('2d');
context.scale(devicePixelRatio, devicePixelRatio);
```

Considering this, it seems a wise choice to stick to SVG for as long as possible and pull Canvas out of the hat when many elements need to be drawn or moved around. You might want to keep things simple until they can't be. One not-so-simple case could be the animation of a great many points. Let's look at an example that demonstrates the performance benefits Canvas has by building an element-heavy, animated application first with SVG and then with Canvas.

Visualizing flight paths with Canvas and D3

Data can come with a great many number of individual data points. Maps especially can be the playground for large datasets. While it might be tempting to visualize features of a dataset as individual elements, in explanatory data visualization especially it often makes sense to aggregate data to bring across a single point well. While Canvas allows you to show and animate many points, it is power you might want to use responsibly.

Having said that, it can often be mesmerizing to watch dynamic data unfold as well as bringing across a specific point. Combining user engagement with concise learnings is of course a great plus you should leverage if possible. Considering map data, there are a great many examples of dynamic visualizations with numerous animated elements, such as natural elements like winds or ocean currents, cultural elements like spreading ideas or inventions, as well technical elements like cars, ships, or airplanes. In this section, we will jump on the latter and visualize flight paths.

Our aim will be two-fold. Firstly, we want to build a map visualization with many animated elements – not just for the sake of showing many elements, but the detail we show should facilitate the understanding of the visual. Secondly, we want to compare the performance between SVG and Canvas. We have described it theoretically in a previous section, but let's get practical now.

Here's what we will build:

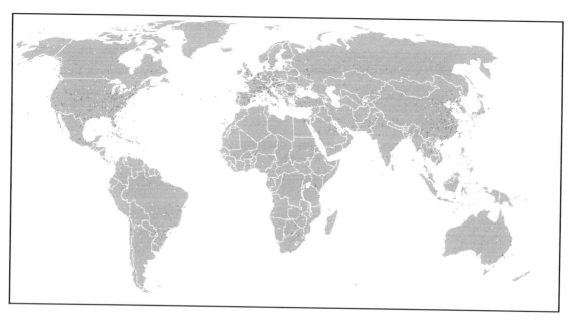

1,000 flight paths visualized. Each red dot is an animated plane (promise!)

There are three main element categories we will draw: *the world, airports* (the white dots, consciously kept in the background as they are of only supporting importance), and the *planes* (the red dots). Representing real planes, our red dots are animated along their very own flight path flying from their origin to their destination. Here's an image showing the paths our planes follow:

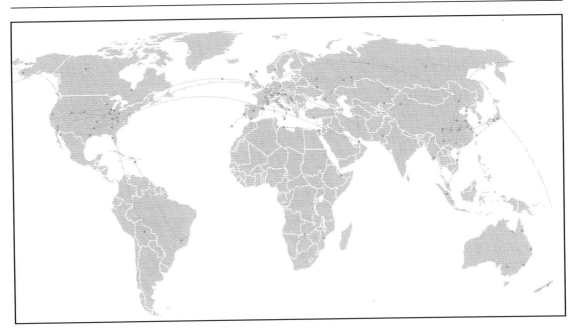

100 flights showing the route paths and their respective planes

The source data for this visual includes over 65,000 worldwide routes flying to and from just over 7,000 airports. We won't be able to animate all these routes, not even with Canvas. The aim of our visualization will rather be to show as many as we can to convey an immediate visual understanding of active versus less active flight regions as well as oft-used versus lesser-used routes.

At the bottom of the visual we will show a row of buttons:

Buttons to kick off the animation

These buttons will allow the user to set the number of flights to be displayed at once. Importantly, this will not be real time or replayed time. We won't bring in any flight schedules, showing flights at the time of day/date they depart or arrive, we will show all flights at the same time! Firstly, this supports the visualization aims described previously and secondly, it will help test performance because as many elements as possible are being animated at the same time.

To test browser performance, we shall add a small information box from `stats.js` at the top left of our app. Once dropped into your code, this nifty info tool displays page performance measures on your page, of which we will be mainly interested in **frames per second (FPS)**. You will see it soon in action, but this is how it looks magnified indicating 60 frames per second:

The data

According to the three element categories we want to represent, we need three data sources to build the visual. The map data, data about airport locations, as well as flight data, showing origins and destinations for each flight. We will call this the **route data**. Both datasets come from `openflights.org` which offers a tool you can use to map flights as well as databases for flights worldwide including routes and airport location data. This is exactly what we're after.

After light cleaning and minor modifications, the first 10 entries of the route data and the airport location data with 100 flights look as follows:

Route data example
route_100.csv

	airline	source_airport	destination_airport	stops
1	LH	IAH	FRA	0
2	PI	ULK	YKS	0
3	AA	SFO	ORD	0
4	G3	SDQ	GIG	0
5	DL	DTW	MSP	0
6	GL	KUS	AGM	0
7	BE	GLA	LSI	0
8	MW	HNL	MKK	0
9	CA	TAO	WUH	0
10	MU	CTU	TXN	0

Airport data example
airport_100.csv

	iata	long	lat
1	YFS	-121.237000	61.760201
2	YMO	-80.607803	51.291100
3	YZF	-114.440002	62.462799
4	SXF	13.522500	52.380001
5	FRA	8.570556	50.033333
6	HAM	9.988230	53.630402
7	MUC	11.786100	48.353802
8	TXL	13.287700	52.559700
9	PAD	8.616320	51.614101
10	LTN	-0.368333	51.874699

The route and the airport data

All variable names are self-explanatory. Note that the first variable in the airport data, *iata*, represents the official three-letter airport code from the **International Air Transport Association (IATA)**. Also note that we had to remove some flights per dataset as not every airport location was available, which in fact leads to a lower number (less than 2-3%) of flights than the buttons suggest.

Building the flight path map in SVG

Our focus in this chapter will be on mapping with Canvas as well as on a benchmark of Canvas against SVG animation. In order to spend our time and effort wisely, I have pre-built an SVG map we can use as a benchmark, leaving us the rest of the chapter to focus on how to build the Canvas flight path app. The chapter is called *Mapping with **Canvas** and D3* after all...

Nonetheless, let's have a quick look at the steps we would take to build this app with SVG. There are roughly eight logical steps to follow:

1. You set up the map with a container SVG, as well as the projection and the path generator for the map
2. You load the map data and draw the map
3. You listen to button events and load in the appropriate dataset depending on the button pressed
4. You draw the airports
5. You calculate each plane's origin and destination position as well as compute a path from origin to destination
6. You sample points along each plane's path and store them in an array (we'll call them *way points*)
7. Using D3, you transition each plane along its path
8. Once each plane has reached its destination, you let the transition start again

Now that we have conjured up our SVG flight path visual, let's see how many planes we can set off without any problems.

Measuring the performance

So here it is – let's make some planes fly. We should start modestly and try with 100 routes:

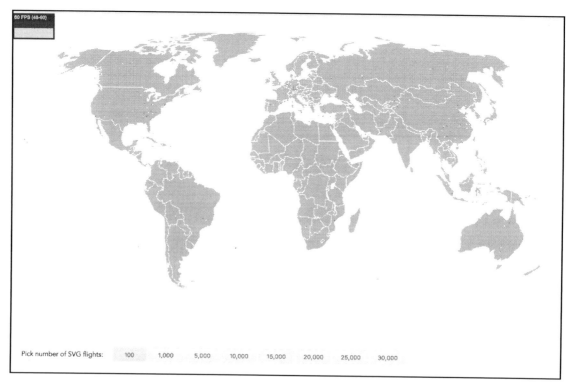

SVG visualization of 100 flight paths at 60 FPS

See the frame rate in the top-left corner? It's a bit small but we're still very happy with it! Displaying 60 frames per second is perfect. 1,000 flights will give us up to 40 frames per seconds. This is a drop, but the animation remains smooth. However, even at 1,000 flights we can't really see any major clusters of flight activity. So, let's try 5,000 flights at the same time:

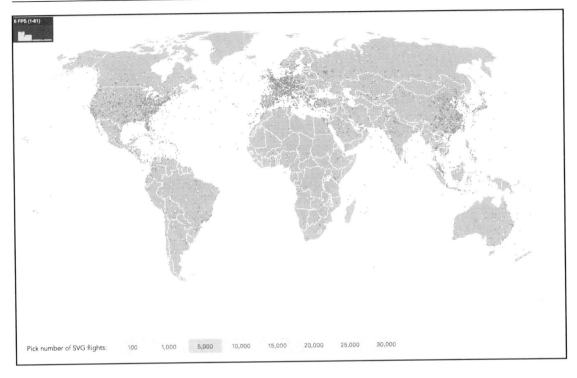

SVG visualization of 5,000 flight paths at 6 FPS

Our performance crashed to 6 FPS. While this static image brings us closer to our visualization aim of identifying regions of high flight traffic, it's no fun to view the janking animation. Canvas to the rescue.

View this step in the browser at: https://larsvers.github.io/learning-d3-mapping-9-1. Code example 09_01.html. I recommend to use a recent version of Chrome to view and work on the examples of this chapter.

At the conclusion of each step you will find two links in an info box close to the the relevant image. The first link brings you to a working implementation of this step that you can view in the browser. The second *code example* link brings you to the full code. If you're reading the print version, you can find all code examples at https://github.com/larsvers/Learning-D3.js-4-Mapping in their relevant chapter.

Building the flight path map in Canvas

Let's start with an overview of our Canvas application before we take it apart.

It's best to quickly get the HTML out of the way as it couldn't be much simpler. We have a div for the canvas at hand as well as our buttons:

```
<div id="canvas-map"></div>
<div id="controls">
    <div class="flight-select" id="button-header">Pick number of
flights:</div>
    <button class="flight-select" data-flights="100">100</button>
    <button class="flight-select" data-flights="1000">1,000</button>
    <button class="flight-select" data-flights="5000">5,000</button>
    <button class="flight-select" data-flights="10000">10,000</button>
    <button class="flight-select" data-flights="15000">15,000</button>
    <button class="flight-select" data-flights="20000">20,000</button>
    <button class="flight-select" data-flights="25000">25,000</button>
    <button class="flight-select" data-flights="30000">30,000</button>
</div>
```

Note that each button gets the same class selector as well as a data-flights attribute to pass on the number of flights each button represents. You will use this in a moment to load the right dataset!

Now let's look at the steps we take in the JavaScript to build this app in Canvas and see what changes to the flow we described previously for the SVG app. I have **highlighted** the parts we change for the Canvas flow and have removed the SVG parts (in brackets):

1. You set up the **Canvas and the context** (instead of a container SVG), as well as the projection and the path generator for the map
2. You load the map data and draw the map
3. You listen to button events and load in the appropriate dataset depending on the button pressed
4. You draw the airports **and the world,** as they are on the same Canvas and a redraw is cheap
5. You calculate each plane's origin and destination position as well as compute a path from origin to destination
6. You sample *way points* along each plane's path and store them in an array
7. **You set off the game loop** (instead of using D3 transitions):
    1. clear the Canvas
    2. update the position
    3. draw the planes

8. In the SVG example we restart a transition, once each plane has reached its destination. In our Canvas app this is part of the **update step in the game loop**.

Setting up the map

First, we set up a few global variables:

```
var width = 1000,
    height = 600,
    countries,
    airportMap,
    requestID;
```

`width` and `height` speak for themselves. Countries will hold the GeoJSON data to draw the globe, which needs to be reached from various function scopes. Hence, it's easier to define it as a global variable in this small app. `airportMap` will allow us to join the airport with the routes data by the three-letter IATA code. `requestID` will be filled by our loop function `requestAnimationFrom()` and used to cancel the current loop. We shall get to this in no time.

We then set up the two contexts: a context for the world and a context for the planes. This little extra work at the beginning makes our life much easier later. If we drew the world and the planes on the same context, we would have to update both the world and the planes every time a plane flies a short distance. Keeping the world on a separate canvas means we only have to draw the world once and can leave that image/context untouched:

```
var canvasWorld = d3.select('#canvas-map').append('canvas')
  .attr('id', 'canvas-world')
  .attr('width', width)
  .attr('height', height);

var contextWorld = canvasWorld.node().getContext('2d');

var canvasPlane = d3.select('#canvas-map').append('canvas')
  .attr('id', 'canvas-plane')
  .attr('width', width)
  .attr('height', height);

var contextPlane = canvasPlane.node().getContext('2d');
```

We use absolute CSS positioning for the canvases to stack them perfectly on top of each other:

```
#canvas-world, #canvas-plane {
  position: absolute;
  top: 0;
  left: 0;
}
```

Next, we set up the `projection`:

```
var projection = d3.geoRobinson()
    .scale(180)
    .translate([width / 2, height / 2]);
```

Please note that instead of playing with `.scale()` and `.translate()` to center and fit your projection, you can use the D3 convenience methods `.fitExtent()` or `.fitSize()`. You pass them your viz dimensions and the GeoJSON object you want to project and it calculates the best scale and translation for you.

Also notice that we don't use the omnipresent *Mercator* projection but the *Robinson* projection for our world map. It has the advantage of drawing the world in a slightly more realistic way in terms of country size proportions. The *Robinson* and many more non-standard projections can be found in the additional *d3-geo-projection module*.

Now we need a path generator. In fact, you will need to build two path generators:

```
var pathSVG = d3.geoPath()
    .projection(projection);

var pathCanvas = d3.geoPath()
    .projection(projection)
    .pointRadius(1)
    .context(contextWorld);
```

`pathSVG` will be used to generate the flight path in memory. We want to do that in SVG as it comes with handy methods to calculate its length and sample points from it. `pathCanvas` will be used to draw our geo data to the screen. Note that we add `d3.geoPath()`'s `.context()` method and pass it our `contextWorld`. If we pass a Canvas context to this `.context()` method, the path generator will return a Canvas path for the passed context. If it's not specified it will return an SVG path string. You can think of it as a switch button to tell D3 which renderer to use.

Drawing the map and listening for user input

As with the SVG process, we start by loading the data in:

```
d3.json('data/countries.topo.json', function(error, world) {
  if (error) throw error;
  d3.select('div#controls').style('top', height + 'px');
  countries = topojson.feature(world, world.objects.countries); // GeoJSON;
  drawMap(countries);
```

We then do a bit of housekeeping and move the buttons in the div#controls below the canvases. You recode the TopoJSON to GeoJSON features and save the data as a global variable before you draw the map:

```
function drawMap(world) {
  countries.features.forEach(function(el, i) {

    contextWorld.beginPath();
    pathCanvas(el);
    contextWorld.fillStyle = '#ccc';
    contextWorld.fill();
    contextWorld.beginPath();
    pathCanvas(el);
    contextWorld.strokeStyle = '#fff';
    contextWorld.lineWidth = 1;
    contextWorld.stroke();

  });
}
```

Thanks to D3's versatile path generator, this is all it needs to draw the world. Easy!

Back in our asynchronous d3.json() data load function, you'll handle the button events next. Remember, nothing has happened yet, but as soon as the user hits a button, the animation should kick off.

You attach a mouse-down listener to all buttons:

```
d3.selectAll('button.flight-select').on('mousedown', handleFlights);
```

Proceed with writing the handler:

```
function handleFlights() {
  d3.selectAll('button').style('background-color', '#f7f7f7');
  d3.select(this).style('background-color', '#ddd');

  if (requestID) cancelAnimationFrame(requestID);
    var flights = this.dataset.flights;
    d3.queue()
      .defer(d3.csv, 'data/routes_' + flights + '.csv')
      .defer(d3.csv, 'data/airports_' + flights + '.csv')
      .await(ready);
}
```

The button colors are handled in the first two lines. The next line will stop the current loop. We haven't even got a loop yet, so let's get back to this as soon as we have.

Finally, we retrieve the number of flights the button represents and load the respective route and airport location data from the server. That's it for the `d3.json()` callback, as the `ready()` function will take over as soon as the data is loaded.

Preparing and drawing with Canvas

With Canvas, we want to achieve three things in the `ready()` function:

```
function ready(error, routes, airports) {
  if (error) throw error;

  // 1) Draw the background scene
  // 2) Calculate plane positions
  // 3) Animate and render the planes
}
```

Drawing the background scene

Before we draw the airports, we manipulate the airport locations data. We create an array holding one GeoJSON point `geometry` object per airport:

```
var airportLocation = [];
airports.forEach(function(el) {
  var obj = {};
  obj.type = 'Feature';
  obj.id = el.iata;
  obj.geometry = {
    type: 'Point',
    coordinates: [+el.long, +el.lat]
```

```
    };
    obj.properties = {};
    airportLocation.push(obj);
});
airportMap = d3.map(airportLocation, function(d) { return d.id; });
```

Then we fill the global `airportMap` variable with a map we produce with `d3.map()`.
`d3.map()` is a utility function that takes an array of objects to produce key-value pairs we
can access with its own `map.get()` method. We won't use the map immediately but will
get to it in a moment.

Every time we call the `ready()` function, that is every time the user presses a new button,
we will redraw airports and the world. Both are drawn on the same canvas. If we want to
change one thing on a canvas, we need to change everything on a canvas. There are ways to
only update regions with clip-paths but with complex animations of multiple elements, this
can become a mess real quick. So we erase and rebuild:

```
contextWorld.clearRect(0, 0, width, height);
drawMap(countries);
drawAirports(airportLocation);
```

Note, we're on the first canvas we've drawn – accessible via `contextWorld`. We've seen
`drawMap()` a few paragraphs ago, `drawAirports()` is even simpler and speaks for itself:

```
function drawAirports(airports) {
  airports.forEach(function(el,i) {

    contextWorld.beginPath();
    pathCanvas(el);
    contextWorld.fillStyle = '#fff';
    contextWorld.fill();

  });
}
```

That's it. This background scene will be drawn with every button press updating the
airports shown.

Defining the planes

Next, we build the fundament for our animation. Essentially, we want an array of points on each plane's route. We will call them **way points** and here's how they will look for the flight path **Frankfurt to Atlanta** as an array and as points on the path:

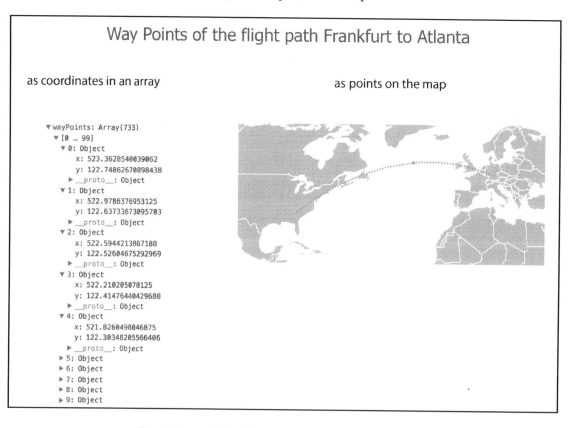

Way points in an array (showing the first 10 of 733) and on the map (an illustration, not exact)

The **way points** are the core ingredient, the fuel for our animation. When we animate the first frame, we will:

1. Clear the plane's own canvas `contextPlane`.
2. Pull out the very first way point for each plane.
3. Draw that plane in this position.

When we draw the second frame we do the same, but in *step 2* pull out the second way point. For the third frame, we shall pull out the third way point, and so on.

We don't want to hold up the browser with complex calculations in between each frame, so we shall calculate all positions for all planes before we animate. Note, this is not always possible, positions might be dependent on user input or arbitrary charges in your force-directed graph or the like. However, whatever you can pre-calculate, you should.

Calculating the plane's positions

How do we get to the `wayPoints` array? Conceptually, we've said it all already. We now express it in code. First, you need to create an array for all planes, depending on the route data the respective button press has loaded in:

```
var routeFromTo = [];
  routes.forEach(function(el) {
    var arr = [el.source_airport, el.destination_airport];
    routeFromTo.push(arr);
  });
```

This is a simple array of elements representing the three-letter origin and the destination IATA airport codes.

Next, you iterate through this array of start and end points to calculate the `wayPoints`. You will create an object called `planes` holding the data as well as two helper functions to calculate the data. But before this, have a look at the simple algorithm to produce the planes:

```
routeFromTo.forEach(function(el, i) {
  var plane = planes.getPlane(el);
  plane.route = planes.getPath(el);
  plane.wayPoints = planes.getWayPoints(plane);
  planes.items.push(plane);
});
```

Conceptually, you produce a plane for each route. Then you get this plane's route path and store it within the plane. Next, you sample the path for a number of *x*, *y* coordinates – our `wayPoints` – and also store it in the `plane`. Lastly, you add the `plane` with all the information you need in the `planes.items` array. That's all the calculation magic in an overview. As soon as that's done, you can animate the points.

Now, let's have a brief look at the `planes` object. Note the plural! This is different to the `plane` object we build for each route. It is the home of all our `plane` objects. `planes.items` will keep all `plane` objects, `planes.getPlane()` will produce them, `planes.getPath()` will create the route's path, and `planes.getWayPoints()` will sample our way points from the path:

```
var planes = {
  items: [],
  getPlane: function(planeRoute) { },
  getPath: function(planeRoute) { },
  getWayPoints: function(plane) { }
}
```

Let's look at what each `planes` function does. There are three simple steps: first, we build the plane, then we draw each plane's path, and finally we sample points from that path we can iterate through to make the plane move:

- **Manufacturing a plane**: the `getPlane()` function takes the `planeRoute` – the three-letter airport codes for origin and destination – and uses it to initialize the plane's position:

```
getPlane: function(planeRoute) {

    var origin = planeRoute[0], destination = planeRoute[1];

    var obj = {};

    obj.od = [origin, destination];

    obj.startX =
projection(airportMap.get(origin).geometry.coordinates)[0];
    obj.startY =
projection(airportMap.get(origin).geometry.coordinates)[1];

    obj.x =
projection(airportMap.get(origin).geometry.coordinates)[0];
    obj.y =
projection(airportMap.get(origin).geometry.coordinates)[1];

    obj.route = null;
    obj.wayPoints = [];
    obj.currentIndex = 0;

    return obj;

}
```

It returns an object holding the `startX` and `startY` positions it retrieves from the `airportMap` lookup you created earlier. It also has `x` and `y` coordinates representing the current position of the plane. For the first frame this is the same as `startX` and `startY`. It also holds an as yet empty object for the `route` path and the `wayPoints` we calculate next. Lastly, it has a `currentIndex` keeping track of the way point the plane is at when we change its position (this will become clearer very soon).

- **Drawing each plane's path**: plane initialized. Now, let's get the path. Remember that we created two path generators during setup? One was a Canvas path to draw worlds, the airport, and plane circles. The other one – `pathSVG` – was for creating the route as an SVG path. Why would you want to do that? Because SVG paths have the great `.getTotalLength()` and `.getPointAtLength()` methods that make it easy to sample points from that path. Here's how to use D3 to create the path:

```
getPath: function(planeRoute) {
  var origin = planeRoute[0], destination = planeRoute[1];
  var pathElement = document.createElementNS(d3.namespaces.svg,
  'path');

  var route = d3.select(pathElement)
    .datum({
      type: 'LineString',
      coordinates: [
        airportMap.get(origin).geometry.coordinates,
        airportMap.get(destination).geometry.coordinates
      ]
    })
    .attr('d', pathSVG);

  return route.node();
}
```

You won't create the path in the DOM, but only in memory and save it in the `pathElement` variable. As it's an SVG and not an HTML element, you need to specify the SVG namespace which you can do with D3's `.namespaces.svg` utility function. Then you create the path before returning the raw element rather than the D3 selection as `route.node()`.

- **Retrieving the way points**: all set to calculate the way points. getWayPoints() takes the plane which by now has its path stored in the plane.route property. We use the path sampling functions we just praised on its path and return an array holding all way points for this specific plane's route path:

```
getWayPoints: function(plane) {
  var arr = [];
  var points = Math.floor(plane.route.getTotalLength() * 2.5);

  d3.range(points).forEach(function(el, i) {
    var DOMPoints = plane.route.getPointAtLength(i/2.5);
    arr.push({ x: DOMPoints.x, y: DOMPoints.y });
  });

  return arr;
}
```

First, you create an empty array called arr which will hold all your way points. Then, you produce an integer saved in the points variable. This integer will represent the number of points we want to sample from the path. You get the total length of the path, which is represented by the number of pixels the path will take up. This, you multiply by 2.5. This very factor is important and controls how many points will be sampled and hence how fast or slow the animation will be. The higher the number, the more points it will sample and the slower the animation will appear. If you choose a low number or even a fraction such as *0.1,* few points will be sampled and the animation will appear faster.

You use d3.range(points).forEach() to retrieve the coordinates returned as so-called DOMPoints by .getPointAtLength() at each point of the path. Then you push each of them into the array and voila, you have your way points.

Congratulations. You have just built a plane. In fact, you have built a plane and its route and all the points you need to make it jump to so that a viewer would think it flies. This is how it looks inside:

```
▼ Object
    currentIndex: 192
  ▼ od: Array(2)
      0: "FRA"
      1: "ATL"
      length: 2
    ▶ __proto__: Array(0)
  ▶ route: path
    startX: 523.362880828818
    startY: 122.74862605929181
  ▶ wayPoints: Array(733)
    x: 448.29803466796875
    y: 108.06956481933594
  ▶ __proto__: Object
```

The plane flying from Frankfurt to Atlanta

Animating the plane

The rest is simple. You just need to apply the game loop to the canvas. We've already encountered this a few times; you create a function called `animate()` and let it run in a continuous loop:

```
function animate() {
  planes.clearPlanes(contextPlane);
  planes.items.forEach(function(el) {
    planes.updatePlane(el);
    planes.drawPlane(contextPlane, el.x, el.y);
  });
  requestID = requestAnimationFrame(animate);
}

requestAnimationFrame(animate);
```

Note, that we added the used functions to the planes object as well, to keep all plane-related function code together.

First, we clear the canvas. `planes.clearPlanes()` literally just clears the context we pass to it.

Then we iterate through the `planes.items` array holding all planes and update each plane with `planes.updatePlane()`. We pass it the respective plane and it either moves the x and y coordinates to the start if the plane has reached its destination or it moves them to the next way point coordinate:

```
updatePlane: function(plane) {
  plane.currentIndex++;
  if (plane.currentIndex >= plane.wayPoints.length) {
    plane.currentIndex = 0;
    plane.x = plane.startX;
    plane.y = plane.startY;
  } else {
    plane.x = plane.wayPoints[plane.currentIndex].x;
    plane.y = plane.wayPoints[plane.currentIndex].y;
  }
}
```

The use of `currentIndex` should become clearer here. It keeps track of where each plane is on its path as well as moving the plane forward by one way point on each update.

Finally, we draw the plane (this is where we realize we haven't built an actual plane but a `tomato` colored circle):

```
drawPlane: function(ctx, x, y) {
  ctx.beginPath();
  ctx.fillStyle = 'tomato';
  ctx.arc(x, y, 1, 0, 2*Math.PI);
  ctx.fill();
}
```

Finally, you kick it off with `requestAnimationFrame()`. You can use `setInterval()` but you should use `requestAnimationFrame()` instead. It will allow the browser to choose the best time to trigger its callback before the next repaint. This is much more economical compared to the brute force `setInterval()`. It also has the additional benefit of interrupting the loop when the browser tab the app runs on is not in focus. Note also, that we save the `requestID` of each loop. You might remember that we use this unique ID to cancel the current loop with `cancelAnimationFrame(requestID)` when the user presses a button to set off a new loop.

Done. Well done.

Measuring the performance

So far so good. But does it work? And if it works, does it work better than the SVG example? Let's recall that the SVG flight path visual gave us a whopping 60 FPS for 100 animated circles and a meager 6 FPS for some 5,000 animated circles. Let's start with 100 circles and focus on the `stats.js` measure in the top-left corner:

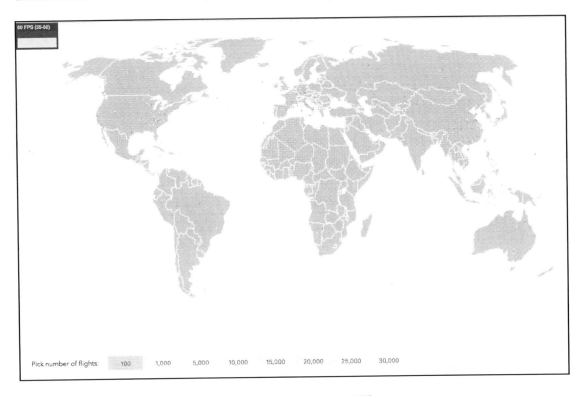

Canvas visualization of 100 flight paths at 60 FPS

View this step in the browser at: `https://larsvers.github.io/learning-d3-mapping-9-2a`. Code example `09_02a.html`.

We expected 60 FPS. Let's go to 1,000 flights:

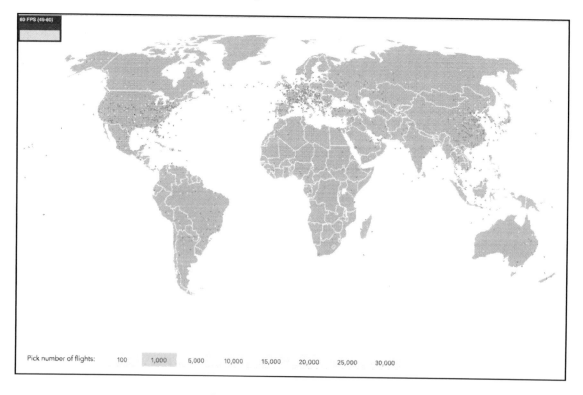

Canvas visualization of 1,000 flight paths at 60 FPS

Again, 60 FPS! 5,000 planes?

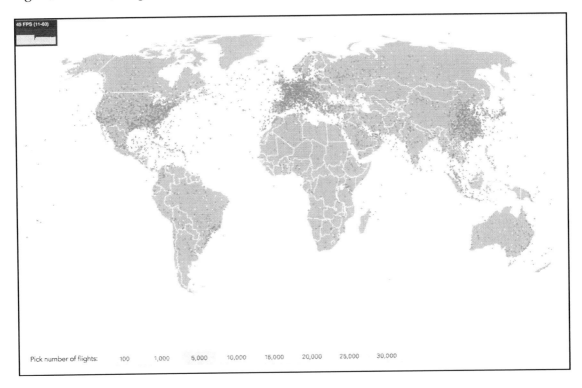

Canvas visualization of 5,000 flight paths at 45 FPS

It's going down, but still at 45 FPS keeping the animation fluid. Let's look at 10,000 flights:

Canvas visualization of 10,000 flight paths at 23 FPS

We still see a frame rate similar to what you see when watching a movie with 23 FPS. However, let's try and squeeze out a bit more.

Optimizing performance

Remember that we've used two canvases for this visual, one canvas to draw the static background scene with the map and the airports and one canvas for the dynamic flight animation. We did this because it kept drawing concerns separate.

Another reason for using an additional canvas is increased performance. We can use one canvas as an **in-memory buffer** to pre-render elements and just copy its contents onto the main visible canvas. This saves render costs as drawing on a visible canvas is less performant than drawing on a non-visible canvas to then copy over the image to the main canvas. Performance further rejoices as the context's drawImage() method we will use to copy over the image from the buffer to the display canvas, is hardware accelerated (meaning it uses the parallel processing powers of the GPU) by default.

For our little app, the animated elements are the plane circles. Instead of drawing them with the `drawPlane()` function for each update, we can first create a single image of a circle on a small buffer canvas and then use `drawImage()` to port it over to the `canvasPlane`.

We create a single plane image in global scope:

```
function createPlaneImage() {
  var planeImg = document.createElement('canvas');
  planeImg.width = planeImg.height = 2;
  var contextPlaneImg = planeImg.getContext('2d');
  contextPlaneImg.beginPath();
  contextPlaneImg.fillStyle = 'tomato';
  contextPlaneImg.arc(planeImg.width/2, planeImg.height/2, 1, 0,
  2*Math.PI);
  contextPlaneImg.fill();
  return planeImg;
}
```

We create our buffer canvas called `planeImg` in thin air, set its `width` and `height` to 2 (double the plane's desired radius of 1), and retrieve its context. We'll draw a `tomato` colored circle on it before we return it.

We call this function once when initializing the `planes` object and store it as an image in the `planes` object:

```
var planes = {
  items: [],
  icon: createPlaneImage(),
  getPlane: function(planeRoute) {
  // ...
```

Finally, we just have to remove our `drawPlane()` function we used to draw the circle on every update. Instead, we add a new function called `drawPlaneImage()` to the `planes` object that uses `drawImage()` to add our plane icon (the circle) to the context we determine:

```
drawPlaneImage: function(ctx, x, y) {
  ctx.drawImage(this.icon, x, y);
}
```

Lastly, we don't call `drawImage()` in the `animate()` function, but `drawPlaneImage()`:

```
function animate() {
  planes.clearPlanes(contextPlane);
  planes.items.forEach(function(el) {
    planes.updatePlane(el);
    planes.drawPlaneImage(contextPlane, el.x, el.y);
  });

  requestID = requestAnimationFrame(animate);
}
```

Continuing with measuring performance

Now let's check the frame rate for animating 10,000 points:

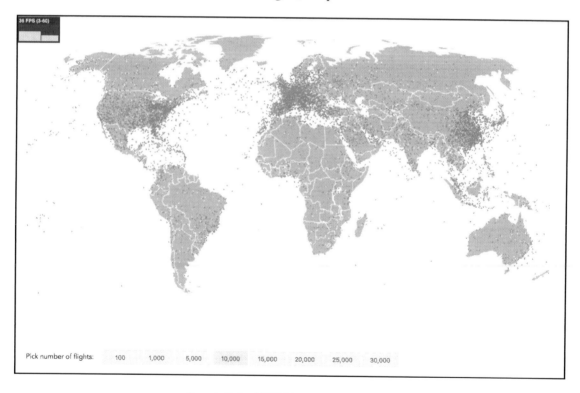

Canvas visualization of 10,000 flight paths at 36 instead of 23 FPS

View complete app at: `https://larsvers.github.io/learning-d3-mapping-9-2b`. Code example: `09_02b.html`.

That's great, boosting performance by about +57% compared to not using the powers of `drawImage()`. It's not shown here, but 5,000 points were animated at 60 FPS instead of 45 FPS. Yay.

Moving on, 15,000 flights fly with 24 FPS and 20,000 with up to 18 FPS. This is still just beyond the 16 FPS generally considered the lowest possible frame rate for fooling the brain into believing a fluid animation. Even 25,000 planes still move with around 14 frames per second conveying a mild jank, while 30,000 flights stutter still only modestly at 12 FPS.

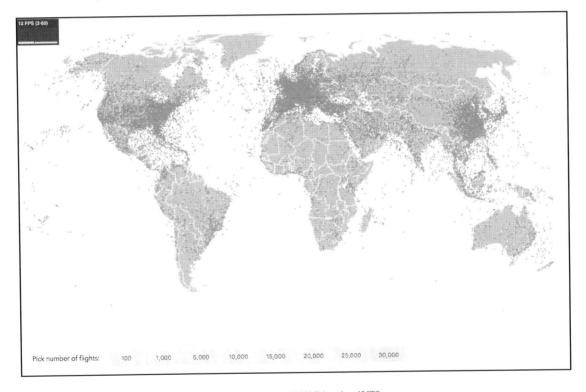

Canvas visualization of 30,000 flight paths at 12 FPS

While performance can vary with different browsers, CPU's and GPU's the jump from SVG to Canvas is significant!

With Canvas we have achieved our narrative mission to visualize regions of heavy flight activity. All of Europe seems to be in the air, as well as the east and west of the US and the east of China. Other continents show a line of increased air-activity along their costs. You might be surprised by the band of planes moving down through Thailand and Indonesia, although this is a densely-populated area.

Summary

In this chapter, you have learned how to build a flight path visualization in SVG and in Canvas, bringing together much of what you have learned before. You have seen how it requires a different mental model to program animations with Canvas, probably best summarized by the game loop: process your data, clear the drawing, re-draw the animation. You have used D3 to set up the visualizations, but you have also seen that due to the different coding concept, Canvas might require you to step away a little from D3 core functionality like transitions. However, all that paid off by witnessing the power of Canvas when it comes to animation. Instead of being able to fluidly animate 1,000 points we managed to animate 15,000 points safely and 20,000 points still gracefully with optimized Canvas techniques.

After having seen the benefits of Canvas, let's now find a workaround for one of its caveats: interactivity!

10

Adding Interactivity to Your Canvas Map

In the preceding chapter, you saw one of the shining qualities of Canvas in action – animating thousands of points on the screen in a smooth animation. In this chapter, you will deal with one Canvas caveat: interaction. While interaction with HTML or SVG elements is straightforward, it requires a little more thought and some tricks to achieve with Canvas. In this chapter, you will follow along these thoughts and learn the tricks needed to do the following things:

- Making a globe move, and adding zoom and rotation interaction to it
- Learning how to interact with Canvas elements through **picking**
- Retrieving data from a Canvas element to display it in a tooltip

After this chapter, you will have covered all important facets of Canvas, drawing, animating, and, finally, interacting with Canvas.

Why Canvas interaction is different

In the preceding chapter, you achieved a smooth animation of thousands of points by doing away with the DOM. The DOM is a representation of each element in browser memory. Bypassing it, you were dealing with much less overhead during animation. However, the DOM can be very useful for other goals in web development. High up on that list – especially for data visualization – is the **interaction** with elements on screen.

You can just add an `onmousemove` or `onclick` listener to an element. You can't do that to elements on a Canvas. They are a pixel manifestation of past code, not represented as a model within the browser.

However, don't despair, there are indirect yet simple techniques to interact with your Canvas. We'll be looking at the most important techniques in this chapter, building an interactive globe:

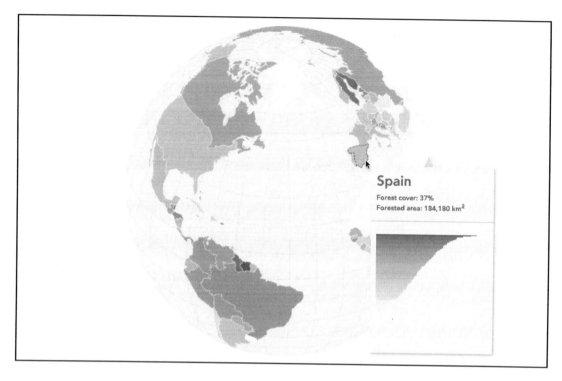

A map of the world's forest cover by country

Leaving flying planes behind, you will build a globe showing each country's forest cover percentage. The greener a country is (you guessed it), the higher the forest cover. As you can see in the preceding figure, you will have a tooltip showing country-specific information when hovering over each country. Users will further be able to rotate the globe and zoom into specific areas at their leisure.

You can view the final app at https://larsvers.github.io/learning-d3-mapping-10-4 **and a** code example at 10_04.html.

At the conclusion of each step, you will find two links in an info box close to the relevant image. The first link brings you to a working implementation of this step that you can view in the browser. The second *code example* link brings you to the full code. If you're reading the print version, you can find all code examples at `https://github.com/larsvers/Learning-D3.js-4-Mapping` in their relevant chapter.

Drawing the world on a Canvas

Let's start drawing a globe. This is straightforward, very much building on the preceding chapter.

Setting up

First, you will create a few variables required for initialization. We'll come back to this list as the application grows, but, for now, it's lean:

```
var width = 960,
    height = 600,
    projectionScale = height / 2.1,
    translation = [width / 2, height / 2];
```

You are setting the `width` and `height` of the Canvas as well as the scale and the translation of the globe. Each projection has their own ideal starting scale. You can play with this number to find the right scale. You will use the `width` and `height` straight away, setting up the Canvas and its context:

```
var canvas = d3.select('#canvas-container').append('canvas')
    .attr('id', 'canvas-globe')
    .attr('width', width)
    .attr('height', height);
var context = canvas.node().getContext('2d');
```

No magic here. Note that we have a `div` with the `#canvas-container` ID in our HTML, in which you add the main Canvas.

Let's also produce a `bufferCanvas`. You learned about the benefits of buffer Canvases in the preceding chapter. In short, rendering an image in memory and copying it onto your main Canvas is more performant than rendering an image directly onto the main Canvas:

```
var bufferCanvas = document.createElement('canvas');
var bufferContext = bufferCanvas.getContext('2d');

bufferContext.canvas.width = width;
bufferContext.canvas.height = height;
```

A rather central part of building a globe is the right projection. Building a globe reduces our options dramatically to the `d3.geoOrthographic()` projection, a 2D globe projection which is part of the standard d3-geo module. You already used it in `chapter 5, Click-Click Boom! Applying Interactivity to Your Map`. Let's set it up first:

```
var projection = d3.geoOrthographic()
    .scale(projectionScale)
    .translate(translation)
    .clipAngle(90);
```

We applied the scale and translation array we specified above, as well as the `.clipAngle()` to 90 degrees to always clip the backside of the projection, our globe.

As we use the `bufferCanvas` for all our drawings, we will tie our projection to a path generator that will exclusively draw to the buffer Canvas , as follows:

```
var bufferPath = d3.geoPath()
    .projection(projection)
    .context(bufferContext);
```

There are two more geo helpers you will create: a base **sphere** and a **graticule**:

```
var sphere = { type: 'Sphere' };
var grid = d3.geoGraticule()();
```

Both are geo-visualization primitives. The **sphere** is, well, a sphere you use to underlay your globe with. You can then fill it or give it an outline to give your globe a round shape beyond the countries. A **graticule** is a grid of the main meridians (longitude lines) and parallels (latitude lines) 10 degrees apart from each other (and, yes, you need four parentheses to produce the actual graticule object). We shall see them in action very soon.

Drawing the world

The scene is set. In this section, you will load some country shape data to draw the world. You will set up four small functions to achieve the draw:

- A `data load` function
- A `ready()` function that prepares the data and passes it on to the render function
- A `renderScene()` function that kicks off the world draw and copies the final image from the buffer onto the main Canvas
- A `drawScene()` function that renders the world onto the `bufferCanvas`.

This might sound overkill for just drawing a static globe, and let me assure you it is. However, we are aiming for higher goals, which will be greatly helped by having this structure set up already.

The data load function just requests the data and passes it on to the `ready()` function:

```
d3.json('../../data/world/world-110.json', function(error, data) {
    if(error) throw error;
    ready(data);
});
```

The `ready()` function doesn't really add much more complexity so far:

```
function ready(world) {
    var countries = topojson.feature(world,
    world.objects.ne_110m_admin_0_countries);
    renderScene(countries);
}
```

It turns the TopoJSON to an array of GeoJSON `countries` and calls `renderScene()`. `renderScene()` does what we've already described in the preceding code. It draws the globe on the `bufferContext` in thin air, and as soon as it's done, copies it over to the freshly cleared main Canvas:

```
function renderScene(world){
    drawScene(world);
    context.clearRect(0, 0, width, height);
    context.drawImage(bufferCanvas, 0, 0, bufferCanvas.width,
    bufferCanvas.height);
}
```

Although `drawScene()` is our longest function, it's not very complex:

```
function drawScene(countries) {

    bufferContext.clearRect(0, 0, bufferCanvas.width, bufferCanvas.height);
    // Sphere fill
    bufferContext.beginPath();
    bufferPath(sphere);
    bufferContext.fillStyle = '#D9EAEF';
    bufferContext.fill();
    // Grid
    bufferContext.beginPath();
    bufferPath(grid);
    bufferContext.lineWidth = 0.5;
    bufferContext.strokeStyle = '#BDDAE3';
    bufferContext.stroke();

    // Country fill
    bufferContext.beginPath();
    bufferPath(countries);
    bufferContext.fillStyle = '#FFFAFA';
    bufferContext.fill();

    // Country stroke
    bufferContext.beginPath();
    bufferPath(countries);
    bufferContext.lineWidth = 0.5;
    bufferContext.strokeStyle = '#D2D3CE';
    bufferContext.stroke();

}
```

It clears the `buffer` context, then draws a base sphere in a light blue and a graticule grid in a slightly more saturated blue. It then fills the countries in a light gray color and strokes each country in a darker gray. That's it. Here's your very own Canvas globe:

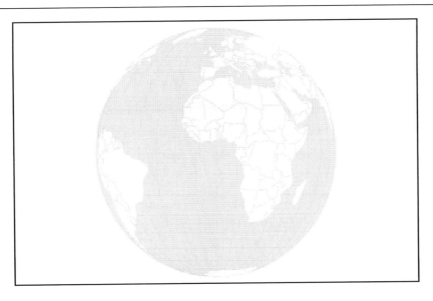

A static Canvas globe

View this step in the browser at `https://larsvers.github.io/learning-d3-mapping-10-1` and a code example at `10_01.html`.

Great! You learned to draw a Canvas globe, which is nice, even if a little mono-dimensional. So, let's add our first bit of interaction with it and let the users (and ourselves) zoom and rotate the globe.

Making the world move

Zooming into and rotating a globe projection is a truly joyous pastime, I find. Apart from being such fun, it's also extremely useful when dealing with globe projections, as the user needs to be able to view the world from different angles.

In this section, we will add our first bit of Canvas interactivity to the globe. We will equip the users with the ability to zoom into and rotate the globe. Apart from setting up two additional global variables, we will exclusively do work in the `ready()` function–our central function tasked to prepare the data. From now onward, it will also deal with interactivity, right here:

```
function ready(world) {
  var countries = topojson.feature(world,
  world.objects.ne_110m_admin_0_countries);
  requestAnimationFrame(function() {
    renderScene(countries);
  });

  /* Interactivity goes here */
}
```

Also, note that we wrapped our `renderScene()` function into a `requestAnimationFrame()` function to always let the browser decide the best time point for a new render.

Note, that here is a prominent and often preferred way to deal with zooming and panning (not so much rotating) in D3 using `context.scale()` and `context.translate()`. However, to implement both zooming and rotating, we won't use these in-built methods, but will change the projection instead. We'll get back to the why a little later as it becomes clear on the way.

Setting up the behavior

Zooming is no more than changing the scale for our projection. Rotating is no more than changing the rotation values of our projection. When you want the user to mandate zoom and rotation, you will need to listen to their mouse movement. As such, you will need to set up a zoom listener to track the user's mouse wheel and drag moves, and attach it to the Canvas. We implemented zoom and rotation already in chapter 5, *Click-Click Boom! Applying Interactivity to Your Map*. In our `ready()` function, as specified above, we will use D3's zoom behavior to deliver all the user interaction changes we need:

```
var zoom = d3.zoom()
    .scaleExtent([0.5, 4])
    .on("zoom", zoomed);

canvas.call(zoom);

function zoomed() { // our handler code goes here }
```

First, you create the zoom behavior with `d3.zoom()`, define scaling bounds between *0.5* and *4*, and inform the behavior to trigger our `zoomed()` handler as soon as a "zoom" event has been triggered. However, so far, this has been a blunt tool. To understand what it does, you have to call it on an element. Call it on your Canvas element, and that element will be the sensor of all zoom-related user events. Importantly, it will listen for mouse wheel and drag events and expose the event information in the global `d3.event` object. It will further store the information in the base element it got called on (in our case, the main Canvas), but we'll be happily served by the `d3.event` object you can tap into at each event.

Further, we want to set up some variables for tracking our scale and rotation whereabouts during zoom. We do this at the very top of our code with the following global variables:

```
var width = 960,
    height = 600,
    projectionScale = origProjectionScale = height / 2.1,
    translation = [width / 2, height / 2],
    projectionScaleChange,
    prevTransformScale = 1,
    rotation;
```

The newcomers in the preceding code are `origProjectionScale`, `projectionScaleChange`, `prevTransformScale`, and `rotation`. Their mission will become clear in the following paragraphs.

Handling zoom and rotation

We set up the zoom behavior, meaning that our Canvas is

1. listening on every mouse wheel and drag
2. firing the `zoomed()` handler on each of these events

Let's now fill our handler to do something to the globe.

What do we want to do? From a bird's perspective, for each zoom, we want to establish the scale for the projection, apply it to the path, and redraw the globe a little bit bigger or a little smaller. For each drag, we would want to establish the new rotation values, apply them to the projection and path, and redraw the globe a little bit rotated. To get there, the handler should distinguish between a zoom and a drag. A zoom should lead to a projection-scale change and a drag should lead to a rotation change. For each path, you calculate the position change. Once that's done, you will need to redraw the globe. It's the game-loop mantra: process user-input, clear the Canvas, then redraw the Canvas with updated data.

Let's start with the zoom action:

```
function zoomed() {
  var event = d3.event.sourceEvent.type;

  if (event === 'wheel') {
    var transformScale = d3.event.transform.k;
    projectionScaleChange = (transformScale - prevTransformScale) *
    origProjectionScale;
    projectionScale = projectionScale + projectionScaleChange;
    projection.scale(projectionScale);
    prevTransformScale = transformScale;
  } else if (event === 'mousemove'){
    // Here goes the rotation logic as this will be triggered upon dragging
  }

  requestAnimationFrame(function() {
    renderScene(countries);
  });
}
```

At first, we will need to distinguish between a zoom and a drag event. D3 makes this easy for us with the d3.event object holding a sourceEvent property specifying what event type the user triggers. If it's a wheel event, we change the scale if it's a mousemove event, we change the rotation. Simple.

Changing the scale looks involved but is pretty straightforward. Before we dive into the code, let's make one important distinction. The projection has a scale, and the transformation upon user zoom also has a scale. However, they are different. Projection scales differ between projections. Our d3.geoOrthographic() projection has an initial scale of around *286* (we set it to *height / 2.1 = 286*). Our transformation has an initial scale of *1*. That's the default.

So, you retrieve the current transformScale via d3.transform.k. You note down the change of this scale to the previous transform scale, which can be negative for zoom in or positive for zoom out. However, as your projection scale is quite a big number (as in *286* to start with) and the transform scale change per zoom will be small (for a normal mouse wheel turn the change might be around *0.005*), you will want to boost this number up to get a noticeable change in your projection. Hence, you will multiply it with a larger number. You can choose any large number you like, but choosing your initial projection scale we called origProjectionScale allows you to port this calculation over to any other projection, and it should work nicely. You then just change the current projectionScale by this projectionScaleChange.

The rest is simple. Just apply it to your globe's projection with `projection.scale(projectionScale)`, set the previous transform scale to the updated transform scale, and re-render the globe. Note, that you don't need to update the path generator, as whenever it's called, it will use the projection as is at the moment of being called, which we've changed accordingly.

That was the hard bit. Rotating is even simpler. You just need to track the changes in the user's mouse movements and apply them to D3's `projection.rotate()` parameters. Let's track the change in mouse coordinates right at the top of the `zoomed()` handler:

```
function zoomed(
    var dx = d3.event.sourceEvent.movementX;
    var dy = d3.event.sourceEvent.movementY;

    // all the rest
```

Note, that the two `MouseEvent` properties `.movementX` and `.movementY` are not available in Safari or Internet Explorer. You can see a cross-browser implementation, which is calculating the two values on the fly in code example `10_02.html` at `https://github.com/larsvers/Learning-D3.js-4-Mapping`.

The rotation logic will trigger when the user drags or rather triggers the `mousemove` event, which goes into the `else if` part of our conditional:

```
if (event === 'wheel') {
    // here goes the zoom logic described previously
} else if (event === 'mousemove') {
 var r = projection.rotate();
 rotation = [r[0] + dx * 0.4, r[1] - dy * 0.5, r[2]];
 projection.rotate(rotation);
} else {
    console.warn('unknown mouse event in zoomed()'); // alerting issues
}
```

In the preceding code, we first retrieve the current rotation values from the projection in the variable `r`. Then, you change the `r[0]`, the yaw value (responsible for rotating the world around its normal or vertical axis) by the *x* change of the mouse coordinates. You further change `r[1]`, the roll value (rotating the world around its lateral axis, going horizontally from left to right) by the y change of the mouse coordinates. We leave the third pitch value as is, and yes, the best way is to throttle these values to a reasonable speed of rotation with `dx * 0.4` and `dy * 0.5`, respectively. Note that this is the straightforward but naive way to rotate the globe. It will fully do in our case. If you want to apply utmost precision, you could use **versor** dragging (check out `http://tiny.cc/versor`). The key difference is that versor dragging rotates the globe in the right direction even when it's upside down.

That's it for rotation. Remember, the world gets re-rendered after this conditional as we do this in the following Canvas game loop: get user input – calculate the new position – re-render.

Here's a static attempt to show dynamic zooming and rotations:

Zooming and rotating a Canvas globe

View the step shown in the preceding screenshot in the browser at `https://larsvers.github.io/learning-d3-mapping-10-2` and its code example at `10_02.html`.

The main benefit of zooming via a projection change is that it allows rotating (that's a win) and guarantees **semantic zooming** of the world rather than **geometric zooming**. When you zoom into a Canvas object with `context.scale()`, it naively enlarges anything that's on the Canvas. So, a country border, for example, gets wider and wider, the more you scale it. That's **geometric zooming**. We, however, want to keep everything constant, apart from the area of the individual country polygons. This is called **semantic zooming**. Another benefit of the **projection change** is that getting the coordinate of a Canvas object by mouse-over is more straightforward. This is our next stop.

Finding the Canvas object under the mouse - Picking

We've done zooming and rotating. Let's celebrate by adding another key piece of interactivity: the mouseover. In fact, we don't want just any mouseover. We want to mouse over an object drawn on the Canvas and retrieve information from that object. Once we have that, we have a lot—we can create tooltips, we can highlight the object, we can link views with another graph showing the same data point, and so on.

Picking, the theory

So, how are we doing this? As established many times above, we can't just add a listener to a set of pixels, because an event is an object maintained by the browser, interacting with DOM nodes. However, our browser doesn't know about the pixel. It doesn't have a representation of the Canvas pixels it wants to interact with. So, how?

The answer is relatively simple: we build it ourselves. Not the DOM, that would be madness, but a representation of our Canvas drawing in which the target object's pixel are charged with this object's information.

So, what do we need to build our own little visual object representation? In short, you will build two Canvases. One **main Canvas** that produces our visual (done already) and one **hidden Canvas** (as in you can't see it) that produces the same visual. The key here is that all elements on the second Canvas will be at the same position in relation to the Canvas origin compared to the first Canvas. We will bend this rule a little in practice, but, for now, imagine that the northern tip of Scotland is at pixel position *250, 100* of the main Canvas and that it is also at *250, 100* of the hidden Canvas.

There is only one key difference between the main and the hidden Canvas. Each element on the hidden Canvas will get a **unique color**. What's more, these color values will be indexes to look up our data values. In our case, we will assign *rgb(0,0,0)* to the first country in our country list: Afghanistan. Our second country will get the color value *rgb(1,0,0)* and so on until our last country–Zimbabwe–will get the color value *rgb(176,0,0)*.

Why? Because, next, we will attach a mousemove listener to the main Canvas to retrieve a flow of mouse positions as we move the mouse. At each mouse position, we can use the Canvas's own method `context.getImageData()` to pick the color of the pixel at this exact position. We just extract the R value from our RGB color and can query our data array to get the object we need.

Our itinerary is clear and, with three steps, relatively short. First, we will create the hidden Canvas. Secondly, we will draw the world with a unique color per country. Finally, we will write the mousemove handler to pick the color and get the data. Lastly, we have to decide what to do with all that data we can access.

Before we start, let's make sure that we actually have some data for each country. Here's our GeoJSON country object that shows the contents of the first two of 177 countries:

```
▼ Object {type: "FeatureCollection", features: Array(177)} 📖
  ▼ features: Array(177)
    ▼ [0 … 99]
      ▼ 0: Object
        ▶ geometry: Object
        ▼ properties: Object
            adm0_a3: "AFG"
            admin: "Afghanistan"
            pop_est: 28400000
          ▶ __proto__: Object
          type: "Feature"
        ▶ __proto__: Object
      ▼ 1: Object
        ▶ geometry: Object
        ▼ properties: Object
            adm0_a3: "ALB"
            admin: "Albania"
            pop_est: 3639453
          ▶ __proto__: Object
          type: "Feature"
        ▶ __proto__: Object
      ▶ 2: Object
      ▶ 3: Object
      ▶ 4: Object
      ▶ 5: Object
      ▶ 6: Object
      ▶ 7: Object
      ▶ 8: Object
      ▶ 9: Object
```

The data properties of the country's array

Our GeoJSON world is a `FeatureCollection` with one feature per country, ascendingly sorted by country name. Each feature is an object holding a `type` property, the `geometry` for the country polygon, and a property called `properties`. In here, we have three data points: the country abbreviation, the country name, and even an estimate of the country's population. Now, let's get to that data by mouse over.

Creating all things hidden

By now, you've set up so many Canvases that, at worst, this code just bores you:

```
var hiddenCanvas = d3.select('#canvas-container').append('canvas')
    .attr('id', 'canvas-hidden')
    .attr('width', width)
    .attr('height', height);

var hiddenContext = hiddenCanvas.node().getContext('2d');
```

The only thing we want to make sure of here is to apply the same width and height that we applied to the main Canvas.

Next, we will draw the world to it. In order to do so, we have to build a projection and path generator and then loop through all countries to draw each country to the Canvas; let's do that:

```
var hiddenProjection = d3.geoEquirectangular()
    .translate([width / 2, height / 2])
    .scale(width / 7);

var hiddenPath = d3.geoPath()
    .projection(hiddenProjection)
    .context(hiddenContext);
```

We, of course, need a new path generator, as we need to feed our now hidden drawing context to the `.context()` method. However–hold on–we already have a projection for the main Canvas. Shouldn't we use it for the hidden Canvas also? Especially, as we said above that ideally the objects on our hidden Canvas should be in the exact same position as the objects on our main Canvas to query the hidden positions easily? However, here, we use an **equi-rectangular** projection, which will draw the world in a rather different way to our **orthographic** projection on the main Canvas. Don't we need the same projection to produce the same globe?

The answer is no, we don't need the same projection. When our mouse is on a specific position on the main Canvas, we just need to find the same position on the hidden Canvas. No doubt, the easiest way to do this is to use the exact same coordinates. However, we can also use the main projection's `projection.invert([x,y])` function to retrieve this position's longitude and latitude values. We will then use the hidden projection to convert the geo-coordinates to pixel coordinates on the hidden Canvas. Long-winded? Yes, a little. However, with a moving object such as a zooming and rotating globe, this saves us from re-drawing the hidden Canvas. We shall see this in action very soon when we build the handler in the third step.

First, let's draw the hidden Canvas.

Drawing the hidden Canvas

There's just a single simple function that does what you need in this step:

```
function drawHiddenCanvas(world) {
  var countries = world.features;
  countries.forEach(function(el, i) {
    hiddenContext.beginPath();
    hiddenPath(el);
    hiddenContext.fillStyle = 'rgb(' + i + ',0,0)';
    hiddenContext.fill();
  });
}
```

The only argument—`world`—is our GeoJSON feature collection. `countries` pulls out just the array of country information, including the polygons and the additional data we're after. We loop through all of them, drawing each country with the `hiddenContext` and — most importantly—we gave each country a color using the `rgb(<country index>, 0, 0)` pattern.

Here we have it! A graph-like structure of our Canvas visual, representing our data.

So far, it's only a function, so let's invoke it. We only need to call `drawHiddenCanvas()` once whenever we have the data available. So, we venture to the `ready()` function and invoke it right after we draw the main Canvas with `renderScene()`:

```
requestAnimationFrame(function() {
  renderScene(countries);
  drawHiddenCanvas(countries);
});
```

Here they are; our two worlds:

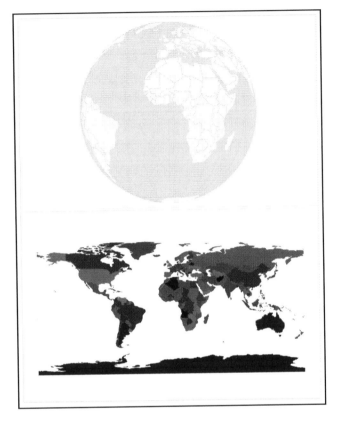

The main and the hidden Canvas

Each country has a slightly different color, ranging from black to red or from *rgb(0,0,0) = Afghanistan* to *rbg(176,0,0) = Zimbabwe*. You can see how countries that start high up in the alphabet—Antarctica, Australia, Brasil, or Canada—are much darker than countries that are low down in the alphabet—the United States or Russia. Note that we'll keep our hidden Canvas visible for demonstration purposes, but, in production, we can just add the CSS rule `{ display: hidden }` to hide our Canvas. No one needs to know about our little trick.

Picking the values

At this point, you have all tools at hands to implement a hover. Now, you will need to make it happen. To wire it all up, you need to do the following steps:

1. Listen to mousemoves on the main Canvas.
2. Translate these coordinates to positions on the hidden Canvas.
3. Pick the color from that position.
4. Strip out the color value that represents the data array index for your data.
5. Lean back and think of ways to use it.

Listening on mousemove is easy; you just need to perform the following command:

```
canvas.on('mousemove', highlightPicking);
```

Done. The first thing we will do in `highlightPicking()` is translate the mouse position on the main Canvas to the coordinates on the hidden Canvas:

```
function highlightPicking() {
  var pos = d3.mouse(this);
  var longlat = projection.invert(pos);
  var hiddenPos = hiddenProjection(longlat);
```

We first get the *x*, *y* mouse coordinates. This will be updated whenever we move the mouse. An example value of the `pos` variable is *[488, 85]*, which is in the north of France. We use D3's own `projection.invert()` which is the inverse of `projection()`. What does `projection()` do? It takes an array of [longitude, latitude] values and returns a pair of [x, y] pixel coordinates. Well, `projection.invert()` does the opposite. It takes a pixel coordinate array and returns the respective longitude and latitude array. In our case, that will be [2.44, 48.81]. The longitude is a bit further right of *0*, which is Greenwich, so yes, that seems right. Note, that this projection is our main Canvas projection. Next, we use our `hiddenProjection()` function to reproject our `longlat` values to the pixel coordinates of this very place. In our example, `hiddenPos` gets the pixel coordinates [485.83, 183.17] assigned to it. That's the very same spot in the north of France on the hidden Canvas! Exactly what we were after.

To demonstrate this, take a look at the following screenshots:

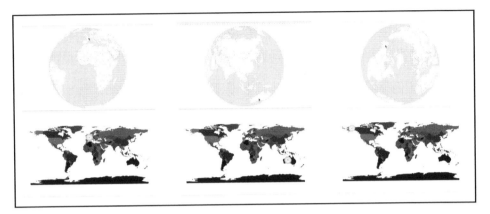

Translating the main Canvas mouse coordinates to the hidden Canvas coordinates

Our mouse position on the upper main Canvas represented by pos gets translated to the lower orange circle represented by the hiddenPos variable.

Now, we finally get to pick that color:

```
var pickedColor = hiddenContext.getImageData(hiddenPos[0], hiddenPos[1], 1,
1).data;
```

This returns a special array with the unwieldy name Uint8ClampedArray representing the R, the G, the B, and the alpha value (peculiarly also ranging from *0* to *255*) at exactly that pixel. In our case, for example, for France (the left most pick in the preceding screenshot), the color is 52:

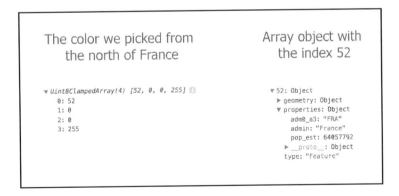

The picked color array

Cross-checking with our `countries` array, we can confirm that the array element with the index 52 is **France**.

However, we will build in two security checks before we can be sure of hovering over a country. First, you will check whether the user's mouse is on the globe and not somewhere in the outer space:

```
var inGlobe =
    Math.abs(pos[0] - projection(projection.invert(pos))[0]) < 0.5 &&
    Math.abs(pos[1] - projection(projection.invert(pos))[1]) < 0.5;
```

In an ideal world, for our purpose, `projection.invert(pos)` above would return `undefined` or similar when we move beyond the globe; however, it still returns actual pixel coordinates, which is not what we want. The problem is that `projection.invert()` is not **bijective**, meaning it can in fact return the same *[long, lat]* coordinates for different pixel position inputs. This is especially the case when we move the mouse beyond the globe bounds. To alleviate this issue, we do a so called **forward projection** here. This just means that we project the inverse of our projection. We take in the pixel coordinates, translate them to *[long, lat]* values and project them back to pixel coordinates. If our mouse is within the globe, this will return our exact mouse position (in fact we give it a leeway of +/- 0.5 pixels here). If our mouse is outside the globe, the forward projection will deviate from our mouse position in pixel.

The second check we perform is to make sure that our mouse is over a country and not a country border:

```
selected = inGlobe && pickedColor[3] === 255 ? pickedColor[0] : false;
```

Let's take this one by one. `selected` will hold the index. You will, however, only get the index if the user's mouse is inside the globe (`inGlobe === true`). This is our first check. Secondly, the fourth element of our special `pickedColor` array has to be exactly *255*. Otherwise, selected will be false. This second check is to surpass **antialiasing** effects.

Why do we need that? The problem with pixels in browsers is that they outsmart us. Lines are feathered at the edges to allow the impression of a smooth transition from line to background:

An aliased line above an antialiased line

Picking values at these feathered edges would not return fully opaque colors, but transparent values of varying degree. These values have an alpha channel lower than 255, so checking for our alpha to be 255 allows us to pick only from aliased areas.

Fabulous! We've built ourself a second Canvas that functions as a memory of the objects on our main data. Next, we'll use it. The Canvas way of changing anything with our elements and objects is to pass the information to the redrawing part of our app to use it in there accordingly.

Storing more data and using a lookup array

We are blessed with the fact that the world we visualize only has 176 countries. This way, we only need to keep track of 176 indeces. However, you often deal with more data objects so that 256 (as in 0-255) will be used up rather quickly. Luckily, we not only have R but also G and B values and their unique combinations, which gets us to $256*256*256 = 16,777,216$ possible indeces you can store. That will bring you far.

Check the tutorial at http://tiny.cc/d3-canvas for more details.

Highlighting the country on mouse over

Whenever a country is picked, we just pass the selected variable through to our `drawScene()` function that draws the world at each mouseover:

```
// ...
selected = inGlobe && pickedColor[3] === 255 ? pickedColor[0] : false;

requestAnimationFrame(function() {
  renderScene(countries, selected);
});

} // highlightPicking()
```

At the end of our highlight handler, we didn't only pass the `countries` to our render function, we also sent our newly created `selected` on the way. The `renderScene()` function just passes it through to `drawScene()`, which draws the world to the `buffer` Canvas. Remember that `renderScene()` just calls `drawScene()`, then clears the main Canvas and copies the `buffer` image over to the main Canvas.

In `drawCanvas()`, we will add a single block:

```
function drawScene(countries, countryIndex) {
  // Clear ...
  // Sphere fill ...
  // Grid ...
  // Country fill ...
  // Country stroke - each country ....

  // Country stroke - hovered country
  if (countryIndex >= 0) {
    bufferContext.beginPath();
    bufferContext.setLineDash([4,2]);
    bufferPath(countries.features[countryIndex]);
    bufferContext.lineWidth = 1;
    bufferContext.strokeStyle = '#777';
    bufferContext.stroke();
    bufferContext.setLineDash([]);
  }
}
```

We will receive the `selected` index via the `countryIndex` argument and check whether it's larger or equal to *0* (remember, that would be *Afghanistan*). If so, we draw a dashed path around the country. How do we know which country? We access the right country via `countries.features[countryIndex]` and draw it accordingly. The mind boggles:

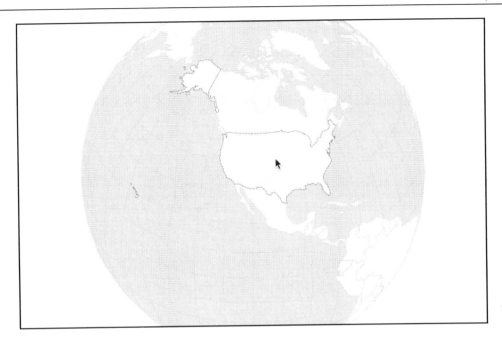

A dashed line around the US, just because we picked the right color

 View this step in the browser at `https://larsvers.github.io/learning-d3-mapping-10-3` and the code example at `10_03.html`.

Visualizing data per country and adding a tooltip

You learned to build a data-driven and -giving representation of your visual. You have also used it to highlight the country at hover. However, you haven't really tapped into the plentiful options of interaction this gives you. Let's do this now. There's a lot you could do, but I think a tooltip would be a reasonable place to start.

Before we embark on the tooltip build, let's add some more interesting data to the globe. So far, we have **country name**, **country name abbreviation**, and **population estimate**. That's already something to work with. However, let's task ourselves with adding an additional data source to our globe, visualize it appropriately, and add a sensible interaction for user exploration.

As a little reminder, this is what you will build:

Our final Canvas adventure

 View the final app at `https://larsvers.github.io/learning-d3-mapping-10-4` and the code example at `10_04.html`.

The preceding screenshot shows a globe visualization of forest cover per country. The data comes from the source of all solid wisdom, Wikipedia. The suggestion is to visualize it as a choropleth map. Arguably, choropleth maps have been overused in recent years, but they are nonetheless a great option to show percentage comparisons of geo-areas.

 The data is from `https://en.wikipedia.org/wiki/List_of_countries_by_forest_area`. The missing North Cyprus, Somaliland, and Haiti have been estimated.

The steps are relatively simple. First, we add our forest data to our GeoJSON world object. We'll move on swiftly to color our countries according to the new data, and finally add a tooltip with HTML and SVG.

Adding new data to our old globe

After copying and pasting or scraping the data from Wikipedia, you should save your forest file in a data format of your choice. We saved it in CSV, and as we now have several data sources to load for one visual, we will use `d3.queue()` to wait for both files to load before invoking `ready()`:

```
d3.queue()
  .defer(d3.json, 'data/world-110.json')
  .defer(d3.csv, 'data/forests.csv')
  .await(ready);
```

Then, adapt your `ready()` function arguments and start accordingly:

```
function ready(error, world, forests) {
  if (error) throw error;
```

Leave the country data prep as is (in that we push the world's country arrays into a variable called `countries`) and move on to including the forest data into the world. What we want is this:

```
▼ Object {type: "FeatureCollection", features: Array(177)} ⓘ
  ▼ features: Array(177)
    ▼ [0 … 99]
      ▼ 0: Object
        ▶ geometry: Object
        ▼ properties: Object
            adm0_a3: "AFG"
            admin: "Afghanistan"
            forest_area: 1631
            forest_color: "rgb(255, 255, 228)"
            forest_percent: 0.0025
            pop_est: 28400000
          ▶ __proto__: Object
          type: "Feature"
```

The updated data object we strive for

The properties we need for the coloring and the tooltip are country name (`admin`), `forest_percent`, and `forest_area`. Note, that we also have `forest_color` here. This is the choropleth color for that country. It's often beneficial to have your data in place before the draw. Hefty calculations during redraw can slow down performance and re-render.

The forest CSV country names have been changed to match the exact naming of the countries GeoJSON. This way, you can use the names to join the two datasets. To join the data speedily, we will use **binary search**. Binary search leverages the sorted nature of our countries array to find a country match quickly. In short, it looks at the country name we want to find, and instead of looping through all countries in the GeoJSON, it splits the countries array in two halves and checks whether the search term is in the upper or the lower half. It does that repeatedly until it finds the term. This is much quicker than **linear search** (looping through all data); in our case, around 10 times faster.

You can implement binary search in D3 with d3.bisect() and that's what we shall use. We add the data with a function we call insertForestDataBinary(). We shall add this function call and the function to the data preparation flow in the ready() function:

```
function insertForestDataBinary() {
    var bisectName = d3.bisector(function(d) { return d.properties.admin;
    }).right;
    for (var i = 0; i < forests.length; i++) {
        var indexBisect = bisectName(countries.features, forests[i].country);
        var indexMatch = indexBisect - 1;
        countries.features[indexMatch].properties.forest_area =
+forests[i].area;
        countries.features[indexMatch].properties.forest_percent =
        +forests[i].percent;
        countries.features[indexMatch].properties.forest_color =
        colorScale(+forests[i].percent);
    }
}
```

First, you create a *bisector* function so that D3 knows which variable we want to find a name (d.properties.admin, the country name). You then iterate through all forest objects. Each forest object holds the country (the name we match), forest_percent and forest_area properties. The bisector will search the array and return the index after the matching countries object (or to the .right, as we specified above). Once you have that, you can add the new properties one index position before.

For the last property, forest_color, you need to create a colorScale somewhere in higher scope:

```
var colorScale = d3.scaleSequential(d3.interpolateYlGn).domain([0,1]);
```

Coloring the globe

Note that you have implemented all these changes before you draw the globe. That's great as you can now simply draw it with the new color scheme. The only change is in our `drawScene()` function, filling the `countries` accordingly in a loop:

```
function drawScene(countries, countryIndex) {
  // Clear the rect, draw the sphere and the graticule
  // Country fill - individual

  countries.features.forEach(function(el) {
    bufferContext.beginPath();
    bufferPath(el);
    bufferContext.fillStyle = el.properties.forest_color;
    bufferContext.fill();
  });

  // Draw the country stroke...
}
```

Also, note that we adjusted the sphere fill and the graticule colors a little to work better with our yellow-green country color scale:

A choropleth globe visualizing forest cover ratio per country

Adding a tooltip

Your globe is colored by forest cover. Yellow countries have a low percentage of cover; dark green a higher one. That's already a good clue about how much forest there is proportionally in each country. However, a user might additionally be interested in how high the forest cover is exactly, and how this compares to other countries. You have all the data in your hands, so let's not be stingy, and add the following tooltip:

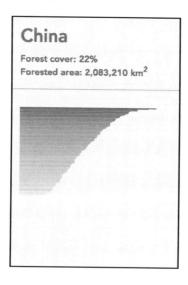

Our tooltip

The visual on the tooltip shows a sorted bar chart of all countries, forest cover percentage, and a red indicator of the hovered country's place in the overall distribution.

The HTML

It is simple, as follows:

```
<div id="tooltip">
  <div id="tip-header">
    <h1></h1>
    <div></div>
  </div>
  <div id="tip-body">
    <svg id="tip-visual"></svg>
  </div>
</div>
```

A tooltip wrapper div, a header with an h1 for the country, and a div to hold the info. The following is a body with an SVG element to hold the bar chart. Note here that we add an HTML and SVG element to a Canvas, which is, of course, no problem. We could even draw SVG elements over the Canvas element or vice versa.

Building the static parts of the tooltip

Next, we will build the tooltip. To be precise, we will build the *static* part of the tooltip, that is, the bar chart. We will add the changing parts such as the header information and the red indicator as soon as we hover over the country. First, we twist the data into the right shape, and then we build a simple bar chart:

```
function buildTooltip(data) {
  var forestsByPercent = data
    .slice()
    .sort(function(a, b) {
      return d3.descending(+a.percent, +b.percent);
    })
    .map(function(el) {
      return {
        country: el.country,
        percent: +el.percent,
        color: colorScale(+el.percent)
      };
    });

  var countryList = forestsByPercent.map(function(el) {
    return el.country;
  });
```

The data we pass into this function is—you guessed it—our forestry-boosted countries' GeoJSON. forestsByPercent is just a sorted array of objects holding the data we need for the bar chart. countryList is just an array of (also sorted) countries we will use as an extension to our ordinal scale. The following is the resulting bar chart:

```
var tipWidth = 200,
    tipHeight = 200;

var xScale = d3.scaleLinear()
    .domain([0, 1])
    .range([0, tipWidth]);

var yScale = d3.scaleBand()
    .domain(countryList)
    .rangeRound([0, tipHeight]);
```

```
        svg = d3.select('svg#tip-visual')
            .attr('width', tipWidth)
            .attr('height', tipHeight);

        svg.selectAll('.bar')
            .data(forestsByPercent)
          .enter().append('rect')
            .attr('class', 'bar')
            .attr('id', function(d) { return stripString(d.country); })
            .attr('x', xScale(0))
            .attr('y', function(d) { return yScale(d.country); })
            .attr('width', function(d) { return xScale(d.percent); })
            .attr('height', yScale.bandwidth())
            .attr('fill', function(d) { return d.color; });

    } // buildTooltip()
```

That was simple. By the way, we build all our interactive tooltip functions in the `ready()`
function. This way, we have access to all the data we need and have it all nicely cordoned
off from any outside JavaScript scopes. In real life, it might be worth considering
outsourcing interactivity to its own module to keep concerns separate.

We call this `buildTooltip()` function in `ready()` after defining an `svg` variable we can
address from the other two tooltip functions, `tooltipShow()` and `tooltipHide()` which
we will build next.

```
    var svg;
    buildTooltip(forests);
```

Showing and hiding the tooltip

We need a small chunk of logic to tell our app when to show and when to hide the tooltip.
With SVG, this logic is usually straightforward, as we can leverage mouseover and
mouseout. With Canvas, we only really have mousemove on the entire Canvas. So, we
build our own mouseover and mouseout logic. We start in the mousemove handler called
`highlightPicking()`:

```
    function highlightPicking() {

      // Here, you find the country index and store it in pickedColor
      // and you check if the user's mouse is in the globe or not with inGlobe

      selected = inGlobe && pickedColor[3] === 255 ? pickedColor[0] : false;
      requestAnimationFrame(function() {
        renderScene(countries, selected);
```

```
    });

    var country = countries.features[selected];
    if (selected !== false) showTooltip(pos, country); // build tooltip
    if (selected === false) hideTooltip(); // remove tooltip
}
```

You store the data of the country the mouse is over in country. If selected holds a number (a country index), we trigger the creatively named function showTooltip() and pass it the main Canvas's mouse positions and the country. If selected returns false, the mouse is not over a country, and we will trigger the equally creatively named function hideTooltip().

The key thing you want to figure out in showTooltip() is when to build a new tooltip and when to just move the existing tooltip. You want to build a new tooltip when the mouse moves from one country to another country. You just want to move the tooltip along with the mouse when the mouse is within the borders of a specific country.

We will achieve this by an array that will work like a **queue**. You can imagine a stack to stand up vertically, able to only add new data to the top or remove data from the top. In contrast, you can imagine a queue horizontally like a queue in front of an ice-cream shop. People arrive in the queue at the back and leave the queue at the front.

Our queue will, however, only be two-people long. In fact, it won't be two people long but two countries long. Whenever we move the mouse, the queue will be fed the country we're over to one side of it (the front actually), immediately pushing off the country at the other side (the back). When we're moving from one spot in the US to another spot in the US, it will say ["United States of America", "United States of America"]. As soon as our mouse moves effortlessly over to Mexico, it will add "Mexico" at the front of the queue, pushing the previously 0-indexed "United States of America" to index position 1 and cutting off the array right there. Now, we have an array with ["Mexico", "United States of America"].

Checking whether we change a country is now a simple affair of comparing the two values in our queue. If they are the same, we just move the mouse; if they are different, we create a new tooltip for Mexico.

This is a textbook example of why SVG or HTML is often preferred over Canvas when the application is interaction heavy. Still, that wasn't too bad, was it? Let's implement it. First, you will need to define your yet-empty queue:

```
    var countryQueue = [undefined, undefined];
```

Then, you need to write `showTooltip()`, taking in the mouse positions and the element, that is, the country the mouse is over:

```
function showTooltip(mouse, element) {
  var countryProps = element.properties;
  countryQueue.unshift(countryProps.admin);
  countryQueue.pop();
```

You save the country's data in `countryProps`, add the country's name to the front of the queue with JavaScript's own `.unshift()` method, and `pop()` off the last value from the queue.

Then, we will establish if there is a country change or not:

```
if (countryQueue[0] !== countryQueue[1]) {
  var headHtml =
    'Forest cover: ' + formatPer(countryProps.forest_percent) + '' +
    '<br>Forested area: ' + formatNum(countryProps.forest_area) + '
    km<sup>2</sup>';

  d3.select('#tip-header h1').html(countryProps.admin);
  d3.select('#tip-header div').html(headHtml);

  svg.selectAll('.bar').attr('fill', function(d) { return d.color; });
  d3.select('#' + stripString(countryProps.admin)).attr('fill',
'orange');

  d3.select('#tooltip')
    .style('left', (mouse[0] + 20) + 'px')
    .style('top', (mouse[1] + 20) + 'px')
    .transition().duration(100)
    .style('opacity', 0.98);
```

If there is one, you fill the tooltip's header with the country-specific information. You also color all bars according to the appropriate country color before the bar of this specific country gets colored red. The rest is just moving the tip along with the mouse and cranking its opacity up to make it visible.

```
If the queue values are the same, you just move the tip:
  } else {
    d3.select('#tooltip')
      .style('left', (mouse[0] + 20) + 'px')
      .style('top', (mouse[1] + 20) + 'px');
  }
}
```

Remember, showTooltip() gets shown every time the mouse is over a country, and our selected variable gets filled with a country index. If selected is false, we know we're not over a country, meaning that we want to remove our tooltip. We do this with, well, hideTooltip():

```
function hideTooltip() {
  countryQueue.unshift(undefined);
  countryQueue.pop();
  d3.select('#tooltip')
    .transition().duration(100)
    .style('opacity', 0);
}
```

We decided to appropriately allocate undefined to the queue if we're not over a country, so we unshift() it to the front of the queue and pop() off the last value of the array to always keep it in pairs we can compare at the next move. Finally, we will transition the opacity back to zero and it is gone again. That's it! All done.

Summary

You have officially seen and used Canvas. You've reveled in its shining moments and mastered its quirks. You have started with a royal blue rectangle and have now successfully built a whole world, which you can spin, resize as desired, and retrieve country-specific information from. On the way, you have also seen how Canvas works in comparison to SVG. You have learned about the benefits and issues when coding a little closer to the graphics processing part of your machine.

The idea of these chapters has, of course, been to extend your technical skill set. However, beyond that, it's the alternative concept of how to approach Canvas—the procedural style, the game loop routine, and the way Canvas interacts with D3—that broadens your horizon as a developer and allows for a different perspective to tackle problems.

11
Shaping Maps with Data - Hexbin Maps

Different pieces of data afford different visualizations. When you want to show a timeline, you rarely build a vertical bar chart. You would more likely use a horizontal line chart. You should, of course, give yourself some freedom of expression when encoding data to position, shape, or color. However, the data at hand, the meaning you want to convey, and the cognitive decoding processes at play are important guides when deciding how to encode your data.

In this chapter, we will focus on a specific map-visualization technique: **hexagonal binning maps (hexbin maps)**. We will start with a brief journey through various map visualization techniques before focusing on hexbin maps. You will learn the conceptual and cognitive benefits of hexbin maps, what hexagons are useful for in comparison to other shapes, and how they are calculated.

Most of the chapter will, however, be hands on, building a hexbin map from scratch. Most of the attention will go into data preparation and shaping. D3 will make the actual visualization a breeze with the **D3-hexbin** module. We will focus on a pipeline of data preparation and visualization tasks that aim to be easy to follow. Let's go!

Reviewing map visualization techniques

There are many ways to represent geographical data. Not surprisingly, maps are often involved. While maps are a compelling way to present data that can be deciphered effortlessly by most people, they can be overused. If you want to show which country has the highest percentage of forest cover, you might decide to show a globe and use color saturation to encode forest ratio. Alternatively, you could show a sorted vertical bar chart displaying the country with the highest forest cover on top and the country with the lowest at the bottom. The map version might look nicer and give your users a good intuition about locations of forest lack or riches. However, the bar chart gives a more concise overview over the distribution and country comparison of forest cover.

So, let's assume that you have decided to use a map as the fundamental representation of your visual. What options are there?

Choropleth maps

Widely known and potentially overused choropleth maps are a good choice if you need to compare standardized ratios across geographical units such as states, counties, or countries. You built a choropleth map in chapter 4, *Creating a Map* and in chapter 10, *Adding Interactivity to Your Canvas Map* comparing forest cover ratio per country

The only visual channel you can encode your measure of choice with is color. The areas of the units are already given by the size of these units. This can draw the user's attention away from the smaller, and toward, the larger units. Looking at our forest example, larger countries such as the US, Russia, or Brazil might get more initial attention than smaller countries, such as Luxembourg, Haiti, or Belize.

To alleviate this attention problem, you should be fair to each country in the measure you visualize. The key rule is to not visualize absolute numbers, but standardized ratios related to the country. We adhered to this rule in our forest example by visualizing the percentage of forested area of the total country area. This measure has the same range for each country, independent of the country's area (0 to 100%). It's a standardized, and hence, fair measure. The absolute number of trees would be an unfair measure. A large country with a few trees could still have more trees than a small country full of trees, rendering our comparison problematic to pointless.

Furthermore, the geographical unit should define the measure you visualize. Tax rates, for example, are made by countries and make perfect sense to compare across countries. Forest cover is not (entirely) informed by a country's actions and policies, and makes less sense to show in a choropleth. The countries' actions still influence their forest cover, so I wouldn't disregard it (the Dominican Republic, for example, has a much more conservative approach to its forests than neighboring Haiti), but this should be a conscious part of your choice of visualization technique.

As choropleths are so omnipresent, let's take a look at another example with different data: farmers' markets in the US. They will accompany us for the rest of the chapter, so this is a good time to dive into it.

The *farmers' markets* data we will use is published by the USDA at `https:/` `/www.ams.usda.gov/local-food-directories/farmersmarkets`. After a bit of a clean up, we have a dataset of 8,475 markets on mainland US. Each market has a number of interesting variables, starting with longitude and latitude values we can use for the mapping, as well as name, state, and city they are located in. It also has 29 binary variables (as in yes/no) indicating the products that each market is selling. We will use this later to visualize subsets of markets.

Here's a choropleth of the US states (only mainland to keep it simple). It shows the number of farmers' markets per 100,000 people. Light blue means few markets; dark blue means many markets per 100k people:

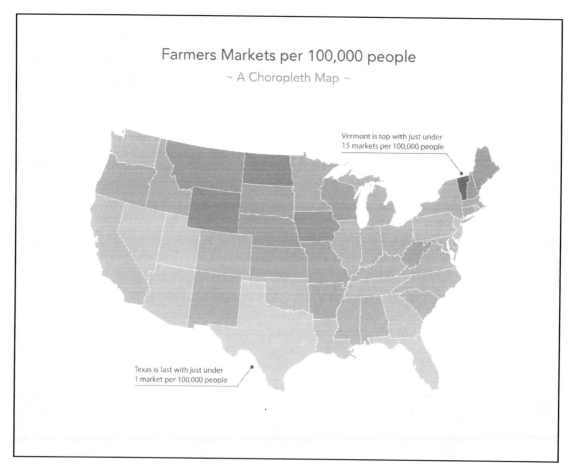

A choropleth map of farmers' markets

One question here has to be whether a state-wise comparison of farmers' markets makes much sense. Do the state-policies or cultures play a role in promoting or objecting to farmers' markets? Maybe. However, once we decided to go for a state-wise comparison of it, are we able to compare well? Texas with its size gets a lot of weight in the visual, suggesting southern farmers' market deprivation. We can see Vermont has the highest ratio (it helps that we're pointing a red line at it), but what about Washington, D.C.? There are 8.5 markets per 100k people? We can't even see it on the map.

Cartograms

Cartograms do away with the area problem, by encoding your values to area size. A cartogram of our farmers' markets mapping the ratio to color and area size would look as follows:

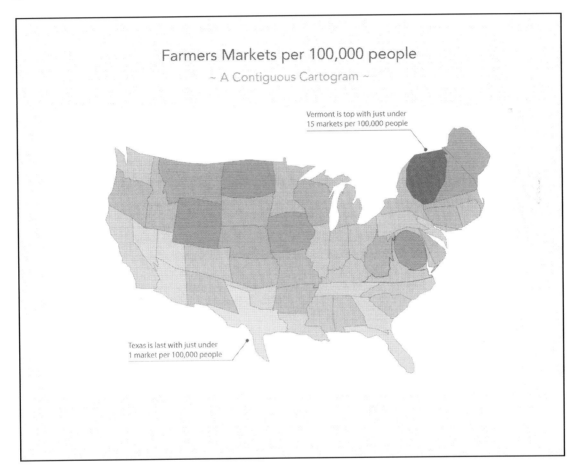

A contiguous cartogram of farmers' markets

The area— and consequently the shape—of your map gets distorted in such a way that the area represents the value you want to visualize. It's great for Washington, D.C. which has been sized up significantly to be recognized as a farmers' markets heavyweight. In short, they solve the choropleth problem of attention theft, but create a new problem in that our geographical units are often hardly recognizable. Your users will be fine with this reality bend for counties, states, and countries they know well, but they will struggle to make sense of areas they don't know the shape of. It'll look too cryptic and reduce readability to a potential full loss of interest.

 The contiguous cartogram has been produced with `https://github.com/shawnbot/topogram`.

Dot density maps

Dot density maps are great if you want to show **counts of things** rather than ratios. Each thing is a dot displayed on the map. Here's a dot density map of all farmers' markets in the US:

A dot density map of farmers' markets

The benefit of this visualization technique is obvious: it shows all the data. You can easily see where they all are and detect clusters of farmers' markets across the country. The problem is that in fact it doesn't show all the data. Some of the dots are overlapping in small, busy areas. A second potential problem is that many absolute measures in spatial analysis correlate highly with population distribution. So while you want to say *Look where all the farmers' markets are* you are actually saying *Look where all the people are*. This doesn't mean you shouldn't show it, but you should be aware of it. By the way, our hexbin map will have the same problem, so be aware. Another caveat of showing all the data is that it might appear confusing for users to look at that amount of data and elements. We might want to focus the eye in a more orderly way to the clusters. This is where hexbin maps come in handy.

Note that this list of map visualization techniques is not complete. There are, of course, other map visualization techniques, such as heat maps, cluster maps, graduated circle, proportional symbol, or bubble maps, and non-contiguous cartograms. A good place to see what people visualize with and on maps is `https://flowingdata.com/category/visualization/mapping/`.

Value and use of the hexagon

Hexagons can solve some of the problems we mentioned in the preceding section. They can help the unequal area problems of choropleth maps and can bring ordered focus to point clusters. Let's look at a few first:

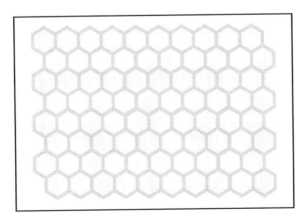

Hexagonal tiling

As you can see, hexagons have equal length sides and fit nicely next to each other. However, they're not just a pretty face, they also have properties we can leverage well in data visualization:

- Hexagons divide a given area into equal-sized hexagons. This is called **tiling** and can also be done with other shapes such as circles, triangles, rectangles, or other polygons.
- However, if you tile your wall with circles, you will end up with gaps between the circles. Covering a plane gap-free with repeating symmetric shapes is called a **regular tessellation** and is, in fact, only possible with squares, triangles, and hexagons.
- Of these three shapes, hexagons are the highest-sided shape closest to a circle. Hence, they are best to represent—to **bin**—a cluster of points. Corner points of triangles or squares are further away from their center than corner points in hexagons, which make hexagons predestined for grouping dot data. Circles are optimal for binning, but then again, they can't be tessellated.

Let's consider binning for an extra moment. **Binning** means grouping data together into equally sized categories. When we have a dataset of 100 people with varying ages, we can look at the frequency of each age, or we bin the data to more digestible age groups, such as 20-39, 40-69, and 70-99. We take individual data points and aggregate them in larger and—usually—equally sized groups.

In a mapping context, we can bin point location data to equally sized areas. Hexagons are well suited for this task as they group points well and also tessellate regularly across the plane. This is what a hexbin map as implemented with D3 can do for you. Instead of potentially piling points on top of each other as we do in dot density maps, we can define hexagonal areas of equal size, aggregating the points to a summary measure encoded with color. As such, **binning** represents the data for each hexagon area potentially better than individual points would do. The **hexagonal tessellation** supports the binning in that it creates the best possible, gap-free, and comparably fair bin shapes.

In the coming sections, we will very much focus on these **hexbin maps**, where each hexagon represents an equal area. Before we dive into hexbins, let's quickly look at another use of hexagons you might have come across: **hexagonal choropleth maps**. The problem the classic choropleth map, as shown above poses, is that smaller states such as Vermont or Washington D.C can easily be overlooked, as they have such low visual weight. Other area-states such as Texas or Montana attract the eye through sheer size. To alleviate this, we can replace the state polygons with hexagons:

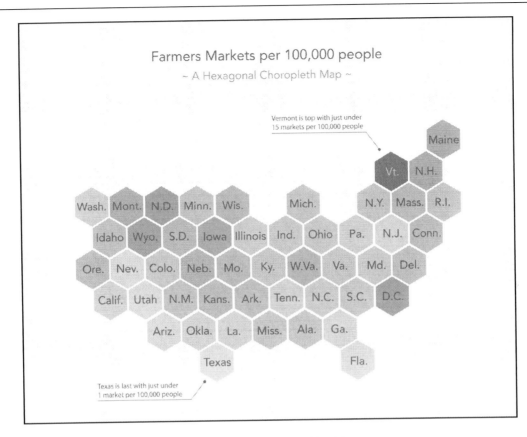

Size emancipated US states in a hexagonal choropleth map

Let's be clear, hexagons in a *hexbin map* as described in the preceding diagram and in the following sections represent equal areas. Hexagons in a *hexagonal choropleth map* as shown in this figure represent vastly different areas. However, in this case, we don't want to focus on the spatial area of our chosen unit (US mainland states); we want to focus on the measure that is merely categorized by our chosen unit.

Be aware that this comes with the cost of removing the area information entirely, as the US states differ greatly in area and no state looks like a hexagon. However, unlike the preceding classic choropleth example, this hexagonal choropleth allows us, for example, to easily identify Washington D.C. as a farmers' market hub and that might be the message we want to bring across above all.

Enough theory. Let's make a hexbin map.

Making a hexbin map

Having improved our US state choropleth map with hexagons, let's now use hexagons to alter our dot density map. There are benefits to a dot density map as we have seen previously, so the changes we are about to make are more alterations than clear improvements. Here's what we will build:

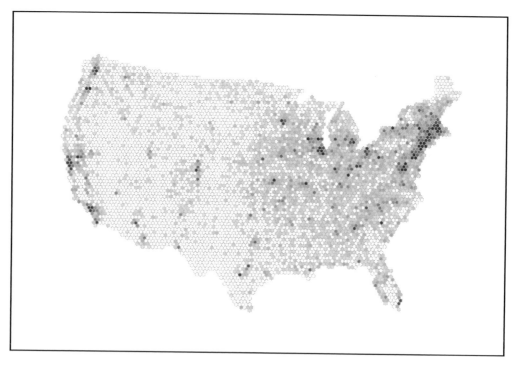

A map of many hexagons in color

It's a hexbin map showing the farmers' markets hotspots. Areas with no farmers' markets are shown as white hexagons, areas with many farmers' markets are shown in blue to dark purple. Lighter and less saturated yellow and green hexagons represent areas with fewer markets.

Reviewing the hexbin algorithm

What do we want to achieve? There are two major steps we want to cover. First, we want to show the US as a hexagon tiling. Next, we want to highlight hexagons with farmers' markets, color encoding the number of markets within each hexagon.

Alternatively, we could be content with showing a map of the US and only display the hexagons where farmers' markets reside. This would be less involved; however, it seems worthwhile to go the extra mile for esthetics and clarity.

The actual drawing of the hexbin is simple, thanks to the d3.hexbin() module doing the hardwork of drawing the hexagons. More attention will be required when producing the hexagonal grid of the US. However, don't worry; the process is straightforward and right here:

1. Draw a map.
2. Overlay the entire map with a symmetric grid of points.
3. Only keep the grid points that are within the bounds of the map.
4. Merge the grid points data with the location data we want to visualize.
5. Calculate the hexbin positions with the D3-hexbin module.
6. For each hexagon, aggregate the summary statistic you want to visualize.
7. Visualize the summary statistic (for example, by color encoding the hexagons):

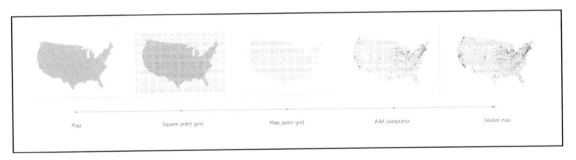

The hexbin map evolution

Setting it up

The setup is simple. You have a single `<div>` with the `id="vis"` in the HTML for the visualization. In the JavaScript, you set up a global `projection` variable to fill soon and create an `svg` element:

```
var projection;

var margin = { top: 30, right: 30, bottom: 30, left: 30 },
    width = 900 - margin.left - margin.right,
    height = 600 - margin.top - margin.bottom;

var svg = d3.select('#vis')
  .append('svg')
    .attr('width', width + margin.left + margin.top)
    .attr('height', height + margin.top + margin.bottom)
  .append('g')
    .attr('transform', 'translate(' + margin.left + ', ' + margin.top +
')');
```

Drawing the map

As usual, the first thing we do is to get your data into the app. So far, you only have the US data; however, in anticipation of the farmers' markets point data, we will haul in a little later—let's use `d3.queue()` to load our data:

```
d3.queue()
  .defer(d3.json, 'data/us.json')
  .await(ready);
```

The `ready()` function gets called asynchronously as soon as the data is loaded:

```
function ready(error, us) {
  if (error) throw error;

  var us = prepData(us);
  drawGeo(us);

}
```

In there, you check for errors, prepare the US data, and draw it. The data preparation is a one-liner, converting the `topo` to an array of GeoJSON polygons:

```
function prepData(topo) {
  var geo = topojson.feature(topo, topo.objects.us);
  return geo;
}
```

The drawing function takes the GeoJSON as its only argument. Create the projection and the path generator and draw the US. `projection` is a global variable as we will use it in other places later:

```
function drawGeo(data) {
  projection = d3.geoAlbers() // note: global
    .scale(1000).translate([width/2, height/2]);

  var geoPath = d3.geoPath()
    .projection(projection);

  svg
    .append('path').datum(data)
      .attr('d', geoPath)
      .attr('fill', '#ccc')
}
```

Note that we are using the `d3.geoAlbers()` projection here. The *Albers* projection is a so-called **equal area-conic projection**, which distorts scale and shape but preserves area. This is essential when producing dot density or hexbin maps to not distort the perceived density of the dots across distorted areas. To put it differently, our hexbins represent equal areas on the projected plane, hence we need to make sure that the projected plane honors equal areas with an appropriate projection. Note that equal area-conic projections require the map maker to pick two parallels (circles of latitude) on which the projection is based. `d3.geoAlbers` has been already preconfigured, picking the two parallels *[29.5, 45.5]*. This produces an optimized projection for the US. When visualizing other countries or map areas, you can overwrite this with the `.parallels()` method or set it up yourself with the `d3.geoConicEqualArea()` projection.

The result is not too surprising:

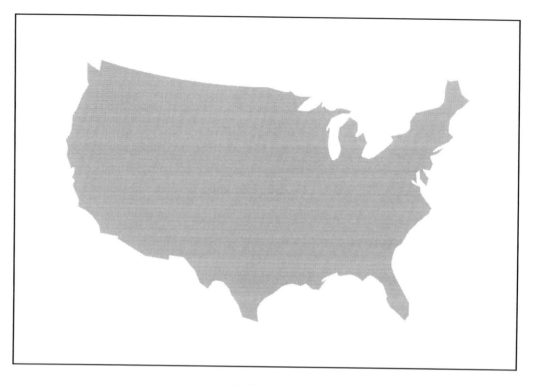

The US mainland

You can view this step in the browser at https://larsvers.github.io/learning-d3-mapping-11-1. Code example ;11_01.html.

At the conclusion of each step, you will find two links in an info box close to the relevant image. The first link brings you to a working implementation of this step that you can view in the browser. The second *code example* link brings you to the full code. If you're reading the print version, you can find all code examples at https://github.com/larsvers/Learning-D3.js-4-Mapping in their relevant chapter.

Before we move on, let's take one step back and look at how we produced the *TopoJSON* data on the command line. The original US map data comes in a shapefile from `https://www.census.gov/geo/maps-data/data/cbf/cbf_nation.html` and is converted from shapefile to TopoJSON in six steps as follows:

1. Install `shapefile`, if you haven't yet:

   npm install -g shapefile

2. Install `topojson`, if you haven't yet:

   npm install -g topojson

3. Convert the shapefile to GeoJSON:

   shp2json cb_2016_us_nation_20m.shp --out us-geo.json

4. Convert the Geo to TopoJSON:

   geo2topo us-geo.json > us-topo.json

5. Compress number precision:

   topoquantize 1e5 < us-topo.json > us-quant.json

6. Simplify the geometry:

   toposimplify -s 1e-5 -f < us-quant.json > us.json

   You can read more on command-line cartography at `http://bit.do/cl-carto`.

Drawing a point grid for our hexagons

Our aim is to draw a hexagon grid across the US map. D3-hexbin will do this for us later, but it can only draw a hexagon where there are points. So, we need to feed points to it. These points won't have any information value for our users. They will only be used to produce the layout. As such, we can distinguish two types of points we will need:

- **Layout points** to produce the hexbin tiling
- **Datapoints** to render the color-scaled information

We'll get to the datapoints soon, but at this stage, we're only concerned with our layout points. Once done, you will have produced this wonderfully regular pattern of points stretching across our entire drawing area:

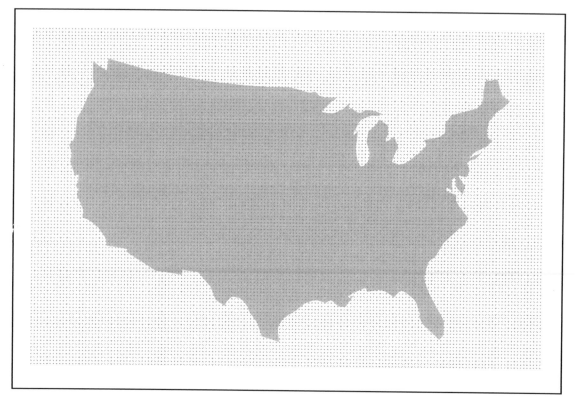

A grid of many points over the US

You can view this step in the browser at `https://larsvers.github.io/ learning-d3-mapping-11-2` and the code example at `11_02.html`.

In the next step, we will cut this grid to shape to fit the US silhouette, but let's lay it out first. Note that this will be the most involved bit of the calculations. No rocket science, but don't worry if it doesn't click immediately. Things often become clearer once stepping through the code in the debugger and/or using a few `console.log()`'s. Anyway, here we go:

```
var points = getPointGrid(160);
```

`getPointGrid()` takes only one argument: the number of columns of points we want. That's enough for us to calculate the grid. First, we will get the distance in pixels between each dot. The distance between each dot stands in for the distance between the hexagon centers. `d3.hexbin()` will calculate this for us precisely later, but, for now, we want to get a good approximation. So, if we decide to have 160 columns of dots and our width is 840, the maximum distance will be *840 / 160 = 5.25* pixels. We then calculate the number of rows. The height is 540, so we can fit in *540 / 5.25* rows, which equals 108 rows of dots if we round it down:

```
function getPointGrid(cols) {
  var hexDistance = width / cols;
  var rows = Math.floor(height / hexDistance);

  hexRadius = hexDistance/1.5;
```

Next, we will calculate the `hexRadius`. This might look funny. Why divide the distance by *1.5*? The D3-hexbin module will produce hexbins for us if we feed it **points** and a desired hexbin **radius**. The hexagon radius we set here should guarantee that the resulting hexagons are large enough to include at least one point of the grid we produce. We want a gap-free hexagon tiling after all. So, a tight grid should have a small radius, and a wide grid should have a wider radius. If we had a wide grid and a small radius, we wouldn't get a hexagon for each point. There would be gaps.

Luckily, hexagons are regular shapes, and their dimensions and properties are nicely interconnected. The vertical distance between hexagon centers is 1.5 times its radius, the horizontal distance is √3 (roughly 1.73):

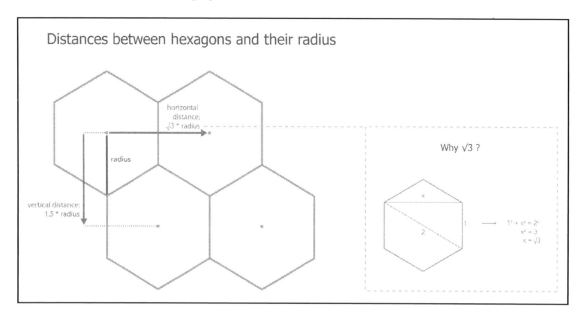

How hexagon distance and radius relate to each other

Our grid points work as a proxy of hexagon centers. As such they are not 'perfectly' laid out in the sense that their vertical distance is the exact same as their horizontal distance with 5.25 pixels. In a perfect hexagon grid the vertical distance would be a little shorter than the horizontal distance as you can see in above figure. In order to get a relatively tight mesh of hexagons on the base of our proxy grid, we should chose a safe—meaning **wide**—radius to pass to the D3-hexbin module which indeed will deliver a perfect hexagon grid. We can calculate this radius with the formulae in the preceding figure as well as our distance (5.25 pixel) by solving for *Radius*. When re-shuffling the equation for the vertical distance *Distance = 1.5 * Radius* becomes *Radius = Distance / 1.5*. In our case the distance is *5.25 / 1.5 =* a radius of *3.5*. Using the horizontal distance would have given us a less safe—meaning tighter—radius with *5.25 / √3 = 3.03*, which in fact would produce a few gaps in our final tiling.

Next, we will create and return the grid immediately—well, the coordinates for the grid that is:

```
return d3.range(rows * cols).map(function(el, i) {
    return {
        x: Math.floor(i % cols * hexDistance),
        y: Math.floor(i / cols) * hexDistance,
        datapoint: 0
    }
  });
} // end of getPointGrid() function
```

`d3.range(rows * columns)` creates an array with one element per dot. We then iterate through each dot with `.map()` returning an object with three properties: x, y, and `datapoint`. These properties will define each of our grid points. The *x* coordinate will increase by the `hexDistance` every point and reset to *0* for each row (or put differently, after it runs through all columns). The *y* coordinate will increase by the `hexDistance` for each new row.

Equally important, each of these grid points will get a property called `datapoints`, which we will set to *0*. This property will distinguish all the layout points (*0*) from the data points (*1*) later, allowing us to focus on the latter.

Congratulations! This was the most difficult bit, and you're still here proudly lifting a square grid of tomato-colored dots into the air.

Note that not crucial but extremely helpful is visualizing the grids and points we make on the way. Here's a little function that draws points if they are stored in an array of objects with x and y properties:

```
function drawPointGrid(data) {
  svg.append('g').attr('id', 'circles')
    .selectAll('.dot').data(data)
    .enter().append('circle')
      .attr('cx', function(d) { return d.x; })
      .attr('cy', function(d) { return d.y; })
      .attr('r', 1)
      .attr('fill', 'tomato');
}
```

Keeping only the points within the map

The square grid of points is still reasonably far away from the shape of the US. Let's change that. Thanks to D3's own d3.polygonContains() method, this is rather simple. The method takes screen coordinates of a polygon and a point, and for each point returns true if the point is in the polygon and false if it isn't. It couldn't be more helpful.

To get the polygon of our US map, we write a small function called getPolygonPoints() and use it as a next step in our ready() function, which so far looks like this:

```
function ready(error, us) {
  var us = prepData(us);
  drawGeo(us);
  var points = getPointGrid(160);
  var polygonPoints = getPolygonPoints(us);
}
```

The only argument we pass in is the array of GeoJSON objects for our map called us. For simplicity reasons, we decided to only look at the mainland US. So, the first thing we need to do is focus our data on the US mainland:

```
function getPolygonPoints(data) {
  var features = data.features[0].geometry.coordinates[7][0];

  var polygonPoints = []
  features.forEach(function(el) {
    polygonPoints.push(projection(el));
  });

  return polygonPoints;
}
```

data.features[0].geometry.coordinates holds 11 arrays of polygon point pairs, describing mainland US as well as Alaska, Hawaii, and further offshore areas. We want to focus on mainland US, whose outline is represented by the first element in the **seventh** array. Note that this might be different if your data comes from a different source or is being assembled differently.

Then, we will loop through all polygonPoints, which are in longitude and latitude, and convert them into x and y coordinates for further use.

Now, we have both the polygon boundaries of the US and our grid points in pixel coordinates. All we need to do now is to identify the grid points that lie within mainland US:

```
var usPoints = keepPointsInPolygon(points, polygonPoints);
```

We pass the two arrays to a function we boldly name `keepPointsInPolygon()`:

```
function keepPointsInPolygon(points, polygon) {
  var pointsInPolygon = [];
  points.forEach(function(el) {
    var inPolygon = d3.polygonContains(polygon, [el.x, el.y]);
    if (inPolygon) pointsInPolygon.push(el);
  });
  return pointsInPolygon;
}
```

In here, we create an empty array called `pointsInPolygon`, which will hold our US-exclusive points. We then loop through our grid points and check for each whether it's within the US polygon or not. If it is, we wave it through into `pointsInPolygon`.

If we were to draw these points, we would see a pointy US:

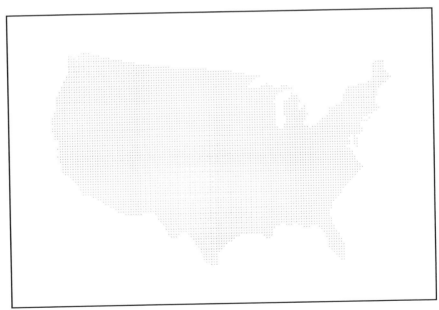

The US in points

You can view this step in the browser at `https://larsvers.github.io/learning-d3-mapping-11-3` the and code example at `11_03.html`.

Making the hex tile

Points are nice and do look pretty, but we're here for hexagons. So, let's finally draw them and introduce the D3-hexbin plugin.

It needs the following two things from us and returns two, surely more valuable, things:

- We need to provide a **set of points** in screen coordinates and the **radius** we would like to see.
- It returns a grid of **hexagon center points** (one for each hexagon) and a **hexagon path generator**.

We then take the new center points and the path generator and—as is custom with D3—draw it ourselves with the renderer of our choice. Let's first get the hexagon center points and then draw them with SVG. In our `ready()` function, we will add the following two lines:

```
function ready(error, us) {
  //previous steps

  var hexPoints = getHexPoints(usPoints);
  drawHexmap(hexPoints);

}
```

`getHexPoints()` retrieves the center points and `drawHexmap()` draws them.

Retrieving the hexagon center points

As mentioned fleetingly previously, `d3.hexbin()` has two heads. Its first use is as a D3 **layout function** such as the force-layout, the tree-layout, or the circle-pack-layout functions D3 offers. Data in, augmented data out. We pass our data and the desired hexagon radius to it, and, for each set of data points it can wrap its shape around, it will return the center coordinate of that hexagon.

If we only gave it one data point, it would return one hexagon. If we gave it two data points close together so it fits into the hexagon's width and height defined by the radius, it would also just return a single hexagon. If the second data point were far off the first one so that the hexagon couldn't cover it with the given radius, d3.hexbin() would produce a second hexagon, embracing that second point.

Here we use its layouting powers:

```
function getHexPoints(points) {
  hexbin = d3.hexbin() // note: global
    .radius(hexRadius)
    .x(function(d) { return d.x; })
    .y(function(d) { return d.y; });

  var hexPoints = hexbin(points);
    return hexPoints;
}
```

First, we configure the layout. We add our radius of 3.5 (the Distance of 5.25 / 1.5) to it and guide its attention to where it can find the x and y coordinates. In the next row, we use it on our grid points and return the resulting array of objects that looks as follows:

```
▼ (5996)
  ▼ [Array(1), Array(1), Array(2), Array(1), Array(1),
    ▼ [0 … 99]
      ▼ 0: Array(1)
        ▶ 0: {x: 126, y: 52.5, datapoint: 0}
          x: 127.30573435631248
          y: 52.5
          length: 1
        ▶ __proto__: Array(0)
      ▼ 1: Array(1)
        ▶ 0: {x: 131.25, y: 52.5, datapoint: 0}
          x: 133.36791218280354
          y: 52.5
          length: 1
        ▶ __proto__: Array(0)
      ▼ 2: Array(2)
        ▶ 0: {x: 136.5, y: 52.5, datapoint: 0}
        ▶ 1: {x: 141.75, y: 52.5, datapoint: 0}
          x: 139.43009000929462
          y: 52.5
          length: 2
        ▶ __proto__: Array(0)
```

Our hexPoints as returned by d3.hexbin()

Our grid points are represented by 5,996 hexagonal center points, which we will just call **hex points** from now on. Let's briefly go through this. The hexbin layout returns an array. Each element represents a single hexagon. In each element, each object represents a point the hexagon covers. Additionally, `d3.hexbin()` adds two keys to the array: x and y. Their values represent the hexagon's center. So, for each hexagon, we have all point data as well as the hexagon's center coordinates.

As you can see in the preceding screenshot, the first two hexagons cover only one grid point, whereas the third covers two grid points. You can also see how the center points in the array keys are slightly different from the layout points in the objects. Let's visualize it.

Drawing the hex tiles

We have our hexagons and now just need to draw them. We do this with a new function we call `drawHexmap(hexPoints)` in our `ready()` function. It does what it says on the tin:

```
function drawHexmap(points) {
  var hexes = svg.append('g').attr('id', 'hexes')
    .selectAll('.hex').data(points)
    .enter().append('path')
      .attr('class', 'hex')
      .attr('transform', function(d) {
        return 'translate(' + d.x + ', ' + d.y + ')'; })
      .attr('d', hexbin.hexagon())
      .style('fill', '#fff')
      .style('stroke', '#ccc')
      .style('stroke-width', 1);
}
```

We join the data (passed in as `points`) with our as yet virtual selection of `.hex` hexagons and use `d.x` and `d.y` to move to each hexagon's center. At each center, we unwrap the second use of our hexbin instance: the **hexagon path generator**. `hexbin.hexagon()` will return the string the path's `d` attribute requires to draw the shape. The dimensions of the hexagon will be based on the radius we have passed to it during configuration. The rest is basic styling.

`hexbin.hexagon()` can also take a radius as an argument. Using an accessor function, we can even pass through a hexagon point-specific argument, meaning that we can change the size of each hexagon based on a data value. Yay! However, we haven't got the time or the data for this now, so let's get back to this later.

Okay, then. Here's your hex tiling; you deserve it:

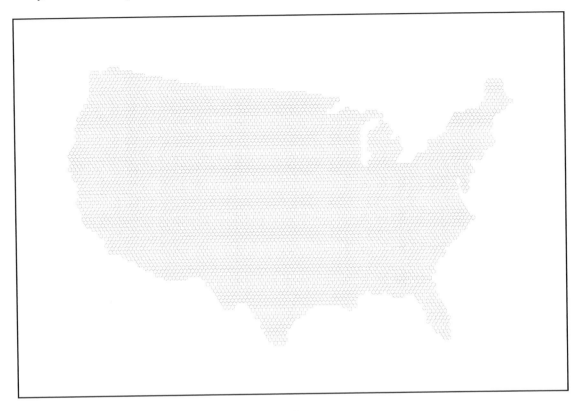

A hextile map

 View this step in the browser at `https://larsvers.github.io/learning-d3-mapping-11-4` the and code example at `11_04.html`.

Joining data points to the layout points

So far, we only had eyes for the base layer setup, visualising our layout points as hexagons. Now, we'll finally add some real data to it. First, we need to load it to our `d3.queue()`:

```
d3.queue()
  .defer(d3.json, 'data/us.json')
  .defer(d3.json, 'data/markets_overall.json')
  .await(ready);
```

In the `ready()` function, we just add another line to our visualization pipeline, triggering a function that will prepare the data for us:

```
function ready(error, us) {
  // ... previous steps
  var dataPoints = getDatapoints(markets)
}
```

`getDatapoints()` simply takes in the loaded CSV data and returns a more concise object boasting *x* and *y* screen coordinates as well as the `datapoint` flag, indicating that this is not a layout point but an actual data point. The rest is market-specific data, such as `name`, `state`, `city`, and `url`, we can use to add as info to each hexagon:

```
function getDatapoints(data) {

    return data.map(function(el) {
      var coords = projection([+el.lng, +el.lat]);
      return {
        x: coords[0],
        y: coords[1],
        datapoint: 1,
        name: el.MarketName,
        state: el.State,
        city: el.city,
        url: el.Website
      }
    });

}
```

Back in the `ready()` function, you just concatenate these data points to the layout points for the complete dataset you will use for your final hexbin map:

```
function ready(error, us) {
  // ... previous steps

  var dataPoints = getDatapoints(markets)
  var mergedPoints = usPoints.concat(dataPoints)
}
```

Here's the markets data visualized as a classic dot density map in blue as well as together with the grid layout data in red:

The left image shows the farmers' markets points; the right image shows the farmers' markets points in blue and layout points in red.

View this step in the browser at `https://larsvers.github.io/learning-d3-mapping-11-5` the and code example at `11_05.html`.

Great! We're one final step away from our hexmap. We need to create a value we can visualize: the number of markets.

Dressing our data for the final act

You have some real data about farmer's markets joined with the hexagons, but you can't use it yet. All your data is still tucked away in the array of objects per hexagon. Let's roll this data up.

The measure we want to visualize is the number of farmer's markets in each hexagonal area. Hence, all we need to do is to count the objects that have their `datapoint` value set to *1*. While we're at it, let's also remove the layout point objects, that is, the objects with `datapoint` value *0*; we won't need them anymore.

We will add our task to the `ready()` function:

```
function ready(error, us) {
  // ... previous steps

  var hexPointsRolledup = rollupHexPoints(hexPoints);
}
```

Primarily, `rollupHexPoints()` will roll up the number of markets per hex point. It will turn the upper hexagon data into the lower hexagon data of the following figure:

The hexagon data before and after roll-up

`rollupHexPoints()` will perform the following things in an order:

1. Remove the layout grid points.
2. Count the number of datapoints and add the count as a new property called `datapoints`.
3. Collect key markets data in single array called `markets` for easy interaction access.
4. Finally, it will produce a color scale we so dearly need for the hexagon coloring.

Here we go:

```
function rollupHexPoints(data) {
  var maxCount = 0;
```

We start by initializing a `maxCount` variable that will later have the maximum number of farmers' markets in a single hexagon. We'll need this for the color scale.

Next, we'll loop through all the layout and data points:

```
data.forEach(function(el) {

    for (var i = el.length - 1; i >= 0; --i) {
      if (el[i].datapoint === 0) {
        el.splice(i, 1);
      }
    }
}
```

First, we will get rid of all the layout point objects with `splice()` if the `datapoint` property holds a `0`.

Next, we will create the rolled-up data. There will be two rolled-up data elements: an integer representing the total count of farmers' markets within the hexagon and an array of market data we can use for later interaction. First, we will set up the variables:

```
var count = 0,
    markets = [];
el.forEach(function(elt) {
  count++;
  var obj = {};
  obj.name = elt.name;
  obj.state = elt.state;
  obj.city = elt.city;
  obj.url = elt.url;
  markets.push(obj);
});

el.datapoints = count;
el.markets = markets;
```

We loop through each object within the hexagon array of objects, and once we've collected the data, we add it as keys to the array. This data is now on the same level as the *x* and *y* coordinates for the hex points.

Note that we could have taken a shortcut to summarize the count of markets. Our `datapoints` property just counts the number of elements in the array. This is exactly the same as what the in-built `Array.length` property does. However, this is a more conscious and descriptive way of doing it without adding much more complexity.

The last thing we do in the loop is to update `maxCount` if the count value of this particular hexagon is higher than the `maxCount` value of all previous hexagons we looped through:

```
    maxCount = Math.max(maxCount, count);

  }); // end of loop through hexagons

  colorScale = d3.scaleSequential(d3.interpolateViridis)
    .domain([maxCount, 1]);

  return data;

} // end of rollupHexPoints()
```

The last thing we do in our roll-up function is to create our `colorScale`. We're using the *Viridis* color scale, which has great properties for visualizing count data. Note that *Viridis* maps low numbers to purple and high numbers to yellow. However, we want high numbers to be darker (more purple) and low numbers to be lighter (more yellow). We will achieve this by just flipping our domain mapping.

The way scales work internally is that each value we feed from our domain will be normalized to a value between *0* and *1*. The first number we set in the array we pass to `.domain()` will be normalized to *0*—that's `maxCount` or 169 in our case. The second number (1) will be normalized to *1*. The output range will also be mapped to the range from *0* to *1*, which for *Viridis* means *0 = purple* and *1 = yellow*. When we send a value to our scale, it will normalize the value and return the corresponding range value between *0* and *1*. Here is what happens when we feed it the number 24:

1. The scale receives *24* as an input (as in `colorScale(24)`).
2. According to the `.domain()` input (`[max, min]` rather than `[min, max]`), the scale normalizes *24* to *0.84*.
3. Next, the scale queries the *Viridis* interpolator about which color corresponds to the value of *0.84* on the *Viridis* color scale. The interpolator comes back with the color #a2da37, which is a light green. This makes sense, as 0.84 is closer to 1, which represents yellow. Light green is obviously closer to yellow than to dark purple, which is encoded as *0* by the interpolator.

That was is it!

Nearly. The very last thing we have to do is to jump into our `drawHexmap()` function and change the hexagon coloring to our `colorScale`:

```
function drawHexmap(points) {
  var hexes = svg.append('g').attr('id', 'hexes')
```

```
  .selectAll('.hex').data(points)
.enter().append('path')
  .attr('class', 'hex')
  .attr('transform', function(d) {
     return 'translate(' + d.x + ', ' + d.y +')';
  })
  .attr('d', hexbin.hexagon())
  .style('fill', function(d) {
     return d.datapoints === 0 ? 'none' : colorScale(d.datapoints);
  })
  .style('stroke', '#ccc')
  .style('stroke-width', 1);
}
```

If the hexagons don't cover any markets, their data points property will be 0 and we won't color it. Otherwise, we pick the appropriate Viridis color.

Here it is:

A very yellow hexbin map

Looks pretty yellow, doesn't it? The problem is that we have a few outliers in our data. That single dark purple dot on the East Coast is New York, which has significantly more farmers' markets than any other area (169). Washington and Boston are busy as well. However, that makes our visual less interesting. Looking at the distribution of numbers tells us that most hexagons enclose 20 or less markets:

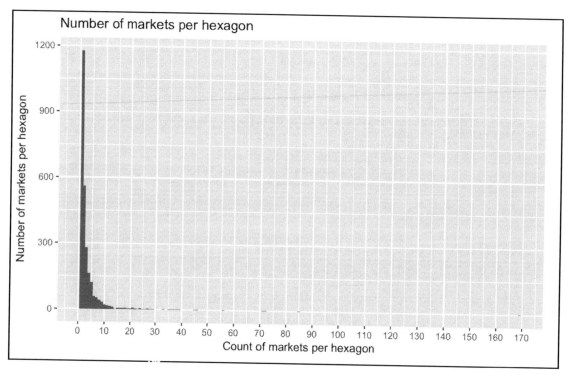

Number of farmers' markets per hexagon

The highest number of markets per hexagon, however, is currently 169. We can do two things here. We can either choose a lower value as our maximum color scale value, say 20. That would only scale our values from 1 to 20 to the *Viridis* spectrum. All hexagons with higher values would receive the maximum colour (purple) by default.

A more elegant alternative is to use an **exponential interpolator** for the color scale. Our domain would map not linearly but exponentially to our color output, effectively reaching the end of our color spectrum (purple) with much lower values. To achieve this, we just need a new color scale with a custom interpolator. Let's take a look at the code first:

```
colorScale = d3.scaleSequential(function(t) {

    var tNew = Math.pow(t,10);
    return d3.interpolateViridis(tNew)

}).domain([maxCount, 1]);
```

What exactly are we doing here? Let's reconsider the scaling steps we went through in the preceding code:

1. The scale receives a number *24* (as in `colorScale(24)`).
2. According to the `.domain()` input (`[max, min]` rather than `[min, max]`), the scale normalizes *24* to *0.84*. No change for points *1* and *2*.
3. With the old `colorScale`, we just waved through this *linearly normalized value* between *1* and *0* without us interfering. Now, we catch it as an argument to a callback. Convention lets us call this `t`. Now, we can use and transform this however we desire. As we saw previously, many hexagons encircle 1 to 20 markets, very few encircle more. So we want to traverse the majority of the Viridis color space in the lower range of our values so that the color scale encodes the interesting part of our data. How do we do this?
4. Before we pass `t` to our color interpolator, we set it to the *power of 10*. We can use a different exponent, but *10* works fine. In general, taking the power of a number between *0* and *1* returns a smaller number. The higher the power, the smaller the output will be. Our linear `t` was *0.84*; our exponential `tNew` equals *0.23*.
5. Finally, we pass `tNew` to the *Viridis* interpolator, which spits out the respective—much darker—color.

Let's graph this transformation to clarify:

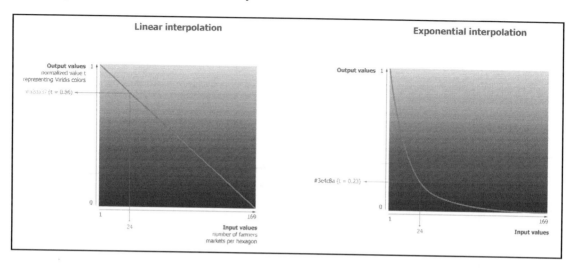

Linear versus exponential color interpolation

The *x axis* shows the input values, the *y axis* shows our scale-normalized value t that we send to the interpolator to retrieve a corresponding color. The **left graph** shows what a linear interpolation does. It linearly translates the increase of values to the decrease in t. The curve in the **right graph** shows us how our adjusted tNew behaves after setting t to the *power of 10*: we enter the lower regions of t (the more purple regions) with much smaller input values. Put differently, we traverse the color space from yellow to purple in a much smaller range of domain values. Piping our example value of 24 through a *linear interpolation* would return a yellowish green; piping it through our *exponential interpolation* already returns a purple value from the end of the color spectrum.

The main win this brings is that color differences can be seen where the data is rather than where the gap between the main data cluster and the outlier is. Here is our hexbin map with an exponential scale:

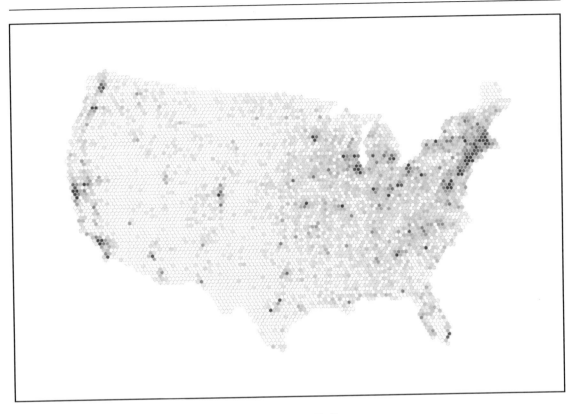

A more interestingly colored hexbin map

 View this step in the browser at `https://larsvers.github.io/learning-d3-mapping-11-6` the and code example at `11_06.html`.

Let's just revel in our achievement for a moment, but are we done? We're itching to explore this map a little more. After all, people are used to playing with maps, trying to locate themselves in them or move from one area to the other with ease. That's what we will allow for in our last step.

Turning our visual into an interactive app

You have officially built a hexbin map, and that was indeed the key focus of this chapter. However, in this last section, let's leisurely consider how we might make this more engaging and informative for ourselves and our users. We won't go into as much detail as in the previous sections, but will go through general steps about how to improve the app.

Here's a list of what we can do:

1. Show the markets in a list on hover.
2. Let the user change the hexagon size.
3. Let the user change the exponent for the color scale interpolator.
4. Show which markets sell specific products, e.g. cheese, wine, seafood, etc.
5. Encode a second variable as hexagon size.

The first is standard. The second and third point would be very helpful for exploration of the data. The fourth point is indeed possible, as the data also covers variables specifying what products each market sells. The last point would be good for our own practice with the d3.hexbin() module.

We won't go into detail of each of these points, but do take a look at the finished app at https://larsvers.github.io/learning-d3-mapping-11-8. The code is commented and available as example 11_08.html in the Chapter 11 folder at https://github.com/larsvers/Learning-D3.js-4-Mapping.

Adding additional information on hover and click

Tooltips are a helpful exploration technique for most visualizations in order to give the user details on a certain data point or area. In this case, the smallest data units of the app are the hexagons. However, some of the hexagons contain more information that would fit on a tooltip—up to 169 as we've seen above. To allow the user to browse the markets per area, we will add a side panel listing all the markets in the hovered hexagon. This is how it could look:

Interactive hexbin map with title, tooltip, and list of markets per hexagon

View this step in the browser at `https://larsvers.github.io/learning-d3-mapping-11-8`. the and code example at `11_08.html`. Please use a recent version of the Chrome browser to view or work along these examples.

The list changes rapidly when the user moves around, so a click on a hexagon would lock the list view so that the user can explore and potentially use the links to get to the markets' websites.

Changing the hexagon size

A key advantage of hexbin maps compared to dot density maps is that interaction is easier. If you have many dots on a map, you might have to keep them small (1-3 pixels) to convey a good sense of the data. Such small targets are hard to catch with the mouse. Furthermore, some dots will inevitably overlap, so you can't get to them at all. In a hexbin map, each hexagon is reachable, if it's not too small. I would even argue that our choice of hexagon size might be a little small with **3.5** pixels. Let's add a drop-down control, allowing the user to change the size of area. Here are some hexagon size variants:

Different hex radii

Two notes of caution here: when building a regularly tessellated hexbin map as we do, you might run into the **border problem**. Imagine a large hexagon just touching the tip of Florida. 5% of the hexagon is over land, 95% is over sea. However, the map readers can't see the real coastal line. They assume the hexagon represents the coastal line, covering 100% land area. If that corner of Florida has a high point density, this hexagon should encode it. However, as it only covers 5% of the land, and maybe around 5% of the dot density, it appears to the reader as though the coast of Florida is void of dots.

Another problem that becomes apparent when you look at the different sized hexagons above is the so-called **modifiable areal unit problem** (MAUD). The summary values we encode are highly dependent on the shape and the scale of our aggregation units. This is a problem, as the results might differ when the same analysis is applied to the same data. You can see the *scale effect* above; changing hexagon size results in a different perception of farmers markets' density. The *shape* or *zone effect* can be more problematic. Using a different shape at the same scale, for example, 10-mile squares instead of 10-mile hexagons can change the aggregate and hence analysis. It then becomes an analysis of different bins rather than of the underlying data. This effect is particularly problematic when representing non-arbitrary units such as counties or census tracts, which might change in shape over time but remain consistent in the readers' minds.

You could solve the border problem by overlaying the country outline, but the key step to alleviate any of these problems is your awareness, explaining potential issues to readers.

Changing the color scale interpolator

In exploratory displays, it can be beneficial for users to change the scale in order to discover data areas of interest. By allowing our users to adjust the interpolator, they can focus on value ranges of their interest. The parameter we want to expose is the exponent our exponential interpolator uses:

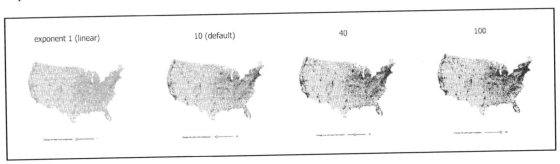

Changing the color scale interpolator

Browsing different datasets

The farmers' market data we are using here also offers over 29 binary variables, indicating what products or facilities markets offer. Multiple datasets showing the geographical distribution of markets with different produce would be a good option. Alternatively, we can add a drop-down menu for the users to choose what products they are most interested in. Here are some examples:

Hexbin maps of different datasets (we chose 20 of the 29 binary variables available for the app)

Encoding data as hexagon size

So far, we have encoded data only as color. `d3.hexbin()` makes it very easy to encode data by hexagon size. Theoretically, you just have to go to your `drawHexmap()` function and change a single line:

```
.attr('d', function(d) { return hexbin.hexagon(d.datapoints); })
```

You just add a hexagon-specific radius to your `hexbin` path generator (as an optional argument to the `.hexagon()` method), which in our case above makes sure that each hexagon gets a radius as little or large as this hexagon's count of farmers' markets. However, that would look excessive as most would get a radius of *0* and some would get a radius of over *100*. I'll spare you the visual.

Instead, we will add the variable `radiusScale` to the mix (in `rollUpHexPoints()`), which will scale sizes from between `3.5` to `15` pixels:

```
radiusScale = d3.scaleSqrt().domain([0, maxCount]).range([3.5, 15]);
```

You can now use it when you draw the hexagons, which you should also sort ascendingly so that the larger ones aren't covered by the many small hexagons around them:

```
function drawHexmap(points) {
  var hexes = svg.append('g').attr('id', 'hexes')
    .selectAll('.hex')
    .data(points.sort(function(a,b) {
        return a.datapoints - b.datapoints;
    }))
    .enter().append('path')
      .attr('class', 'hex')
      .attr('transform', function(d) {
        return 'translate(' + d.x + ', ' + d.y + ')';
      })
      .attr('d', function(d) {
        return hexbin.hexagon(radiusScale(d.datapoints));
      })
      .style('fill', function(d) { return
        d.datapoints === 0 ? 'none' : colorScale(d.datapoints);
      })
      .style('stroke', '#ccc')
      .style('stroke-width', 1);
}
```

You get hexagons not only colored, but also sized by the number of markets within the hexagon:

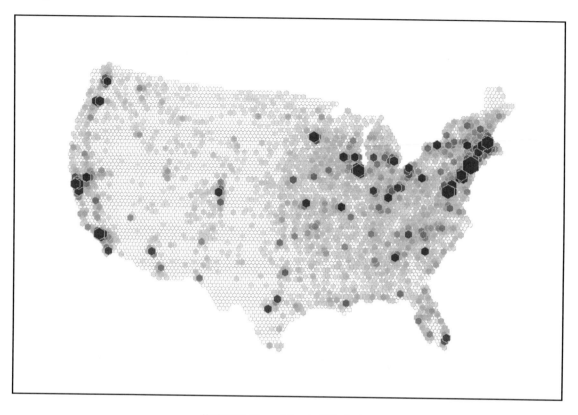

Number of markets encoded as color AND radius size

 View this step in the browser at `https://larsvers.github.io/learning-d3-mapping-11-7` and the code example at `11_07.html`.

We double encode the number of markets as color and size here. That's sometimes useful, but you have two encoding channels at your disposal here, which you can use for two variables to produce a **bi-variate hexbin map**. It's your choice.

We've covered a few options to improve and add to our hexbin map. There are certainly more options to have fun with. For example, we haven't touched on zooming and panning, which is, of course, a standard map interaction technique and would be a good addition for people to dive into smaller hexagons. I'm sure that you can think of more ways to build on it.

Summary

We started by comparing a few map visualization techniques. We covered the uses, benefits, and caveats of choropleth maps, cartograms, and dot density maps. We moved swiftly to the hexagon shape and explored how its geometrical properties can help choropleth and dot density maps.

Most of the chapter was, however, spent in the mapping workshop, building a hexbin map from scratch. We could have built a simple hexbin map, just covering areas with datapoints, but our goal was to shape a map entirely of hexagons for the kicks and the aesthetics. That meant a little more data preparation—creating a map-shaped layout grid, joining the datapoints, and eventually adding and color-encoding the hexagons—but doesn't it look pretty?

Finally, we turned our static map into an interactive application, handing significant control over shape and information gain to the user. A lot can be achieved with interaction, especially with maps!

After having created a fully functional interactive visualization, you might want to show it to the world. There are many ways to claim some online real estate; in the next chapter, we'll look at a conveniently simple one: *GitHub pages*.

12

Publishing Your Visualization with Github Pages

Once done with the hard work of creating your visualization, you should show it to the world, and the internet seems the perfect place for that.

In this chapter, you will learn how to publish your visualization online. There are several ways to do so, stretching from simple command line one-liners using your machine as a server, to full-fledged hosting services that require you to build and deploy a server yourself. We will focus on a simple, fast and convenient way—**GitHub Pages**. Here's what we will cover:

- Get an understanding of Git, GitHub, and GitHub Pages
- Create a GitHub repository with your files and folders
- Upload your files to GitHub and edit them for publishing
- Publish your visualization on GitHub Pages

These are all easy steps, no matter whether you are a seasoned Git and GitHub user or if you have just started out. Let's dive into it.

What we will publish

First, you need something to publish. Let's assume that after mapping so many earthly things, you were reaching for outer space—mapping our solar system:

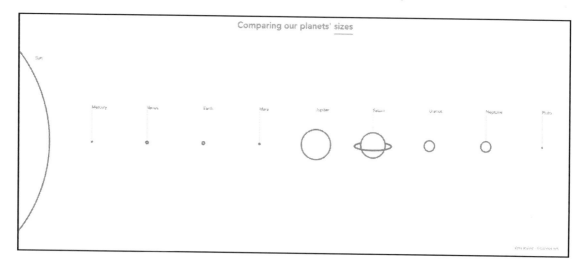

Planets in pink

This visual shows all planets of our solar system in a row, ordered from left to right by their distance to the sun and showing their scaled sizes in relation to each other. It also shows the sun (not a planet, but a star) and Pluto (officially, a dwarf planet).

So, at this stage, you have a visualization in an HTML file or in a set of files stitched together in an HTML or JavaScript file; that's all you need. Your published work is just a few clicks away, thanks to how simple GitHub Pages makes the process.

Feel free to take a peek at the GitHub account we will set up, including the code at `https://github.com/GoodToBeHere/pink-planets` as well as the published visual at `https://goodtobehere.github.io/pink-planets/` or at `planetsin.pink/`.

Understanding the type of content you can publish

Before we jump into it, let's briefly consider what type of content GitHub Pages can host. In short, GitHub Pages will let you serve any **static web page** or pages with **dynamic client-side scripting**. If you want to host projects with dynamic server-side scripting, you might want to opt for a different setup, for example, **Heroku**.

In simple terms, static or flat web pages consist of a set of files—or at least a single HTML file that serves the same content to every user. If you want to change the content, you need to change the source code.

Dynamic web pages consist of a set of files that await external requests or inputs to then build, change, and serve the content on the fly. They might show different contents for different users, or for different times of the day or operating systems.

There are two types of dynamic web pages:

- Web pages with **client-side scripting** usually use JavaScript and its derivatives to translate user input to a changed DOM structure. It does so *client-side*, which means that it happens entirely within the bounds of the browser.
- Web pages with **server-side scripting** require input parameters passed all the way to the application's server. Server-side languages such as PHP, Python, Node.js, or the like assemble the page content in a situation-bespoke way, often with information retrieved from databases.

In short, you can host your project on GitHub Pages if it's not dependent on server-side scripting. You can facilitate user input as long as it happens within the bounds of the client. You can join and update all data that comes from a flat file stored as such on your GitHub page. This can be a `.csv` or otherwise delimited data file, but you can't connect to, for example, a relational SQL database (which relies on structured interrelationships). You can, of course, calculate and recalculate data, as long as it happens client-side.

It is important to be aware of this limitation in order to choose the right hosting technology to publish your visualization. However, many D3 projects in the wild can be hosted as static web pages or dynamic pages with exclusive client-side scripting.

Hosting your code on GitHub

In this section, we'll set you up for the publishing of your visual. We'll explain a few key terms that will help understand GitHub and its purpose; we create an account, upload our content, and prepare it for publishing. This will be a gentle introduction to GitHub. If you already have an account and know about repositories, committing, pulling, pushing, merging, and branches feel free to jump on to the *Publishing your project on GitHub Pages* section.

Making sense of some key terms and concepts

Let's look at some terminology first. If you are a seasoned Git or GitHub user, feel free to skip this introduction.

This is a very high-level introduction to Git and GitHub, and by no means complete. If you want to learn more about Git, I recommend reading the excellent documentation at https://git-scm.com/. If you want to know more about GitHub, https://guides.github.com/activities/hello-world/ is a great place to start.

Git is a **distributed version control system**. Let's break that down. **Version control** of a file (usually a text file such as a .html or .js file) just means keeping track of all the changes made to the file. Before you can use it, you need to download, install, and initialize it in the folder you would like to track files in. Git has three core concepts that make your coding life easier.

Tracking historic changes of your files

Once initialized in a folder, Git allows you to save or **commit** a file to that folder after you changed it. Without Git, you might stoop to making explicit copies of a file you're working on and misusing its name to represent the version such as myFile-v01.html and myFile-v02.html. Instead, Git will assign a commit ID to each commit. Going back through all your commits is easy; just open or check out the version you would like to see. Usually, you don't just version control a single file but many files living in different project folders. The root folder of all the key files you want to version control, the one you initialized Git in, is called the Git **repository**.

Collaborating on a project

The big advantage of Git, as compared to its predecessors, is that it is distributed. It allows many people to access the same project files and each person with granted access sees the full history of versions for each file. It is made for collaboration. To share a repository, it needs to be accessible by some sort of network, for example, the internet. This is where GitHub comes into play.

Assuming that you start a project with the bold goal of visualizing our solar system, you can start coding on your own. You create your own local repository and add and commit the files you want to track in the repository. A few days and many commits later, you realize that this is much too large a task for you to pull off alone. You invite friends to help you. In order to work on the code base together, you upload all your files to GitHub and tie it to your local repository via Git. Git now knows that there is a local repository of your project and a remote repository mirroring the local repository.

Once you have made changes to a file locally and committed them, you can overwrite the same file on the remote GitHub repository by **push**ing this file up. Your friends can **pull** the changes you made down to their local machines and see the exact same files you see, including the file with the changes you just made and all changes made previously.

Working on project branches

You can also maintain parallel **branches** of your project. Each branch is a copy of your project.

Imagine that you have a production version of your project that lives on a website visited by millions of people each day. This production version will be your **master branch**. Now you want to add a new feature; for example, a button that changes the planets' color from pink to purple. You don't want to develop this feature in the production version. This can be dangerous as things might break and your millions of visitors might turn away in disgust. So, you create a copy of your project—a branch you might call the *purple* branch. You can now merrily develop locally, commit different versions of it, and make and fix mistakes. You can push your changes up to GitHub to collaborate with your friends until it works, is tested, and makes you happy. Then, you copy all changes from the *purple* branch to the *master* branch, or better expressed in Git-terminology: you **merge** the purple branch into the master branch.

As said, this can only be a quick tour past the bare bones of Git and GitHub. There's surely more, but being comfortable with these key concepts and terms, you can now confidently set up yourself and your project on GitHub.

Setting up a GitHub account

As setting up an online account is something you have probably done a lot of times in your life, we won't spend much time on this. Here we go:

Setting up a GitHub account

Go to `https://github.com/`, click on **Sign in**, and follow the steps. We express our generally positive attitude to GitHub by choosing the **Username** `GoodToBeHere` and enter our **email address** and a **Password**. On the second screen, we opt for the free account and, after answering a few optional questions on the third screen, we complete our signup.

Creating a repository

Next, we want to set up a repository. Remember that a repository is the root folder of your project holding all your files and folders. There are two ways to create this repository on GitHub:

- You can push up a local repository—a project folder on your local machine
- You can create a new repository online via GitHub

In this chapter, we will only look at the second way and do everything online.

It makes sense to connect your project to GitHub via the command line if you are working continuously with Git and GitHub. It only requires basic familiarity with the command line, and you can learn more about it at `https://help.github.com/articles/adding-an-existing-project-to-github-using-the-command-line/`.

After setting up your account, you will be directed to your very own GitHub dashboard, as you can see in the URL:

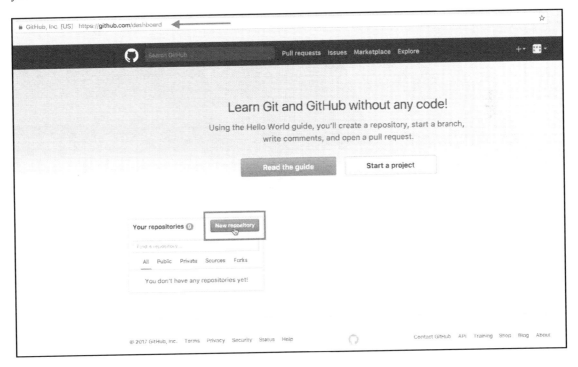

Your GitHub dashboard

To create a new repository, click on **New repository**.

Considering the next screenshot, we will first name our repository. All your repositories will be owned by you, so they will all start with your username. Each repository needs to have a unique name within your list of repositories. For now, you are pretty flexible as this is your first and only repository so far. We'll appropriately call our repository pink-planets, avoiding any spaces in the name:

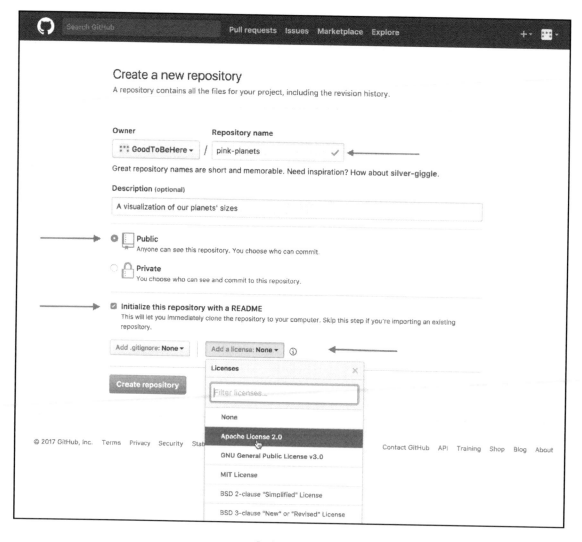

Creating a repository

All our repositories will be **Public**, which means that everyone can see all your code! If you would like or need to keep your code private, you can opt for a paid personal plan.

It's a good practice to initialize the repository with a README file, which allows a description of your project. Don't worry about the .gitignore file, we won't need it here. Lastly, we add a license, in our case, an **Apache License 2.0**. There are several licenses you can choose from, and it's a good idea to make yourself acquainted with the options here.

Lastly, we hit the big green **Create repository** button, which does exactly that and brings us straight to the repository's page:

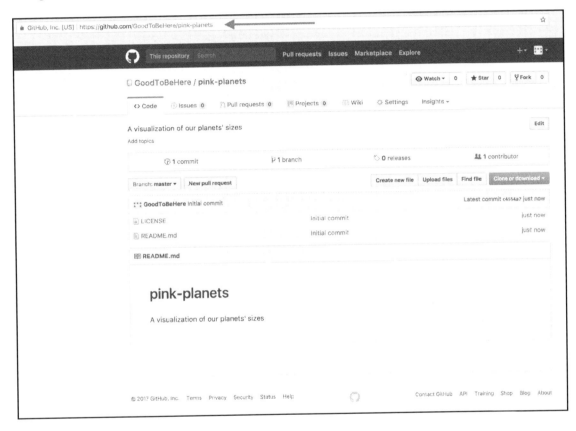

Our repository's page

You can see the name of your repository, a control bar with several tabs displaying the contents of the **Code** tab in focus, and a quick description. Next, there's a bar showing you some general information such as how many commits (or file saves) have been done, how many branches (or project copies) this repository boasts, how many releases there are, and how many contributors have access to this repository.

After the row of button controls, we have a folder view of all files and folders in our repository. Currently, there are only the two files we just created: the LICENSE and the README.md file; .md stands for **markdown**, which allows you to format text files with a simple syntax. You can learn the gist of it within a few minutes at, for example, https://guides.github.com/features/mastering-markdown/.

At the bottom, you see the contents of the README file, giving visitors or collaborators a quick summary of what your project is about.

It's still a little bland, so let's change it and, at the same time, learn how to edit a file via GitHub.

Editing a file on GitHub

If you want to edit a file, you first need to click on its link in your repository. Next, you click on the **Edit this file** pencil in the upper-right corner:

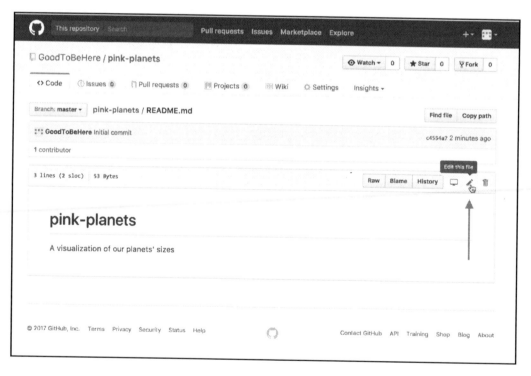

Opening a file for edit

This will direct you to an editable view of the file. In here, you can change the name of the file above the editor window (we leave that as we're happy with README.md as a name), and you can change the file's content in the **Edit file** view:

Changing the README.md file

We've only done a few changes here: we capitalized the title and added some text to describe what the project is about. We're using markdown syntax to mark the headline as headline 1 with the # before the text. We also use markdown to print sun in bold with the prepending and trailing asterisks. The great thing about markdown files is that we can also use normal HTML tags for styling, as we do here with the word dwarfed—writing it in subscript.

Once done with our edits, we can change from the **Edit file** tab to the **Preview changes** tab and see what we've done. The preview marks our changes clearly with coloring and strike-through:

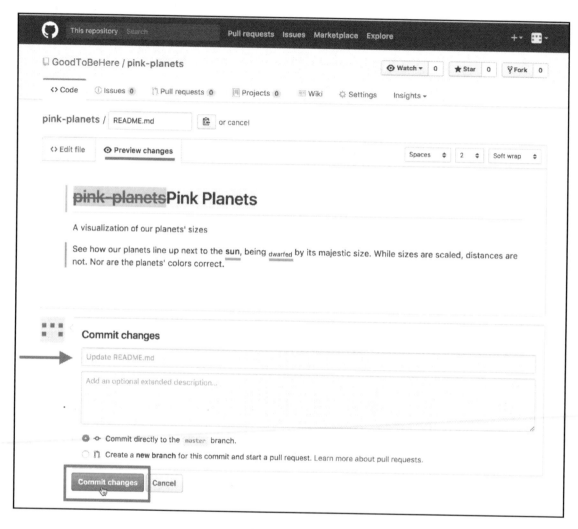

Previewing our changes

We now want to save these changes, which, in Git's language, means **commit**. We can do this with the big green button at the bottom. However, before we do so, we have to add a commit message consisting of a mandatory short summary line and an optional extended description. We can add those to the text fields under **Commit changes**. Think of the commit summary line as an email title and the extended description as the email body.

A good commit summary line is short (less than 70 characters) and completes the sentence *This commit will...*, summarizing concisely what the changes include. GitHub is so kind as to offer us a predefined description depending on the changes we made. In this case, it offers us **Update README.md**, which we're perfectly happy with, so we won't change it. We'll leave the optional extended description field blank, and click on **Commit changes**.

Uploading files to the repository

Let's now upload our project files and folders. Back on our repository page, we find the **Upload files** button:

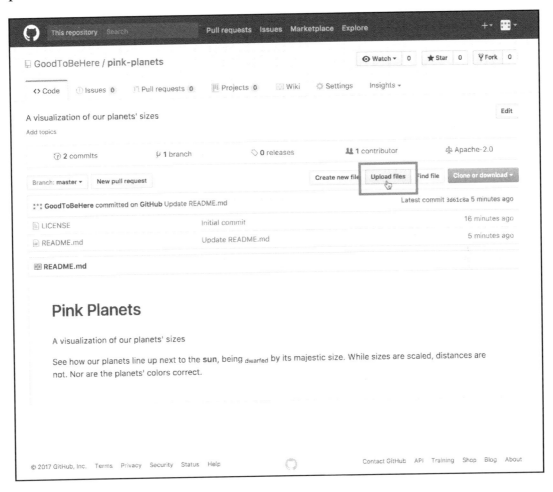

Uploading files

We get to an upload field and drag all our project files over, like this:

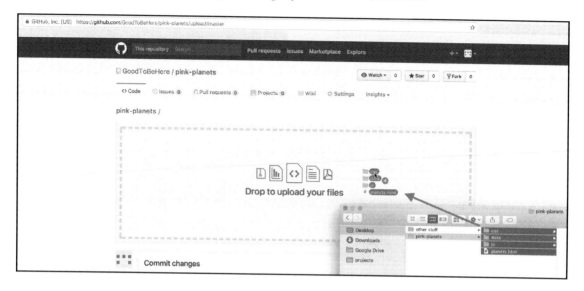

Dragging our files to upload

Our project consists of four files in three folders. We have a `planets.html` file in the root directory, three folders called `/css`, `/data`, and `/js` containing the `planets.css`, `planets.csv` and `planets.js` files. We just grab them from our folder and drag them over.

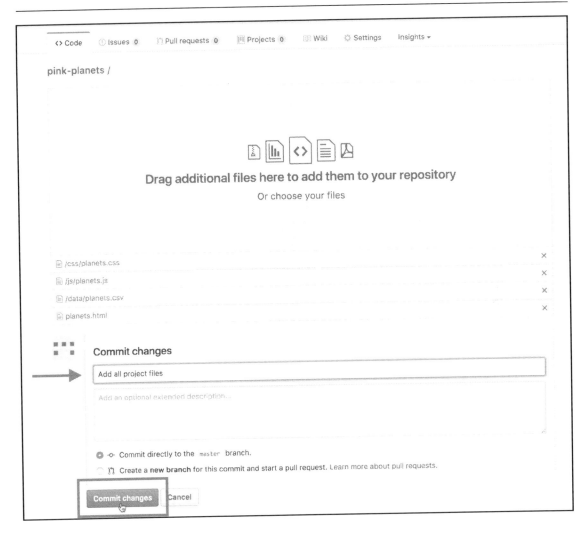

Committing our project files and folders

Once uploaded, we need to commit our changes. We add a short commit message summary and click on **Commit changes**.

We'll be redirected to the repository page and can see all our uploaded files:

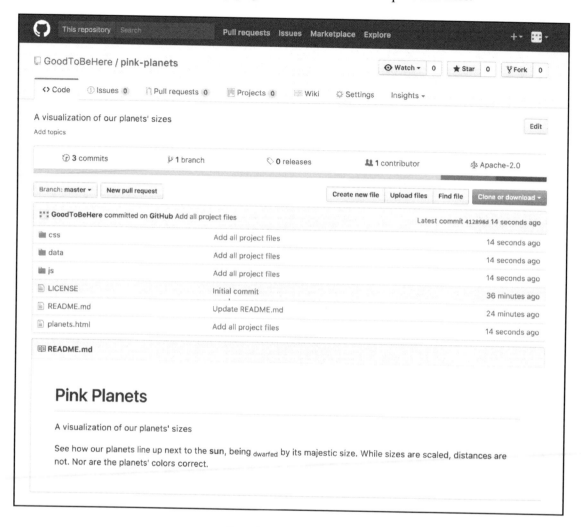

The repository with all our project files

Publishing your project on GitHub Pages

Great, you have your project on GitHub. It doesn't get any more complex. You're just two small preparations and a few clicks away from having your project online!

Preparing the files for publishing

Before we can click on that publish button, we need to ensure that your files are interlinked in the right way, and that your main HTML file is called index.html.

Keeping your paths absolute

First, let's check all our file references. There are two links from within our HTML file, one to our .css file and one to our .js file:

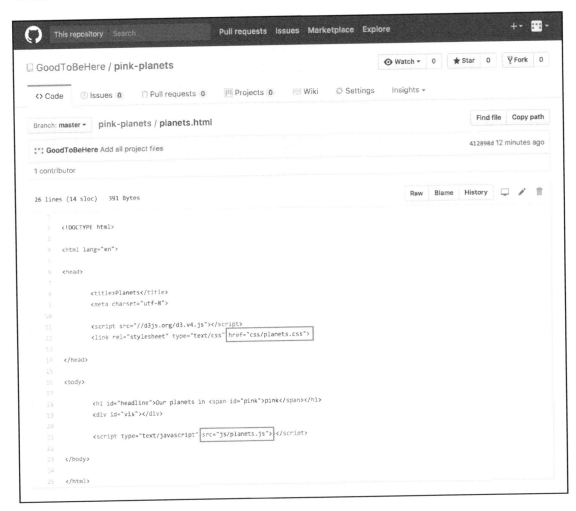

Correct links within the HTML file

All paths on GitHub can be referenced as absolute paths pointing to the root directory. This saves you from working out the relative path from any file at any depth of your directory tree. However, it also means that you might have to change relative paths from your local directory to root-based absolute paths. Your HTML file `planets.html` (we will change this to `index.html` in the next step) lives in the root directory. Both the `css` and `js` folders are also saved in the root directory, so the two paths are absolute to root and will work locally as well as in GitHub.

However, in our project, we're also referencing the `data/planets.csv` file from the `js/planets.js` file. Locally, you may reference this as a relative path, first moving up a level with `../` as in `'../data/planets.csv'`. However, in GitHub, the following will work:

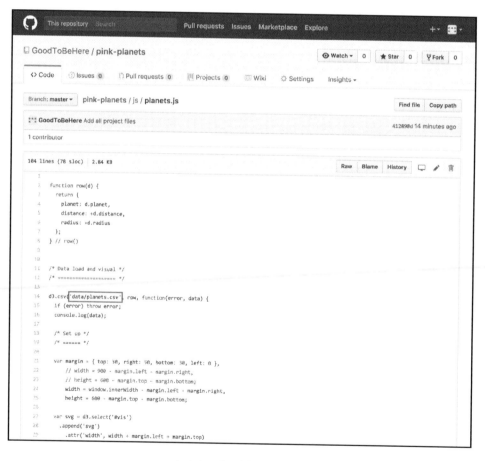

An absolute path used within a nested file

In short, you can always use absolute paths relative to root within your GitHub project.

Changing the main HTML filename to index.html

Your main HTML file might already be called `index.html`. If it's not, just go to the file and rename it to `index.html`, as follows:

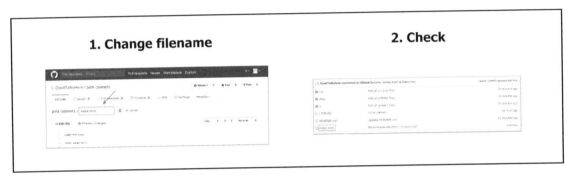

Ensuring that our main HTML file is called **index.html**

Well done, that's all the preparation required. Now, let's publish!

Publishing your project

After all that, erm, hard work, you deserve a simple process to publish. Well, you are exactly five clicks away from viewing your project online. Here they are:

1. Click on the **Settings** tab from your repository home page:

Your repository settings

2. Navigate to the **GitHub Pages** area and expand the drop-down menu in the **Source** field:

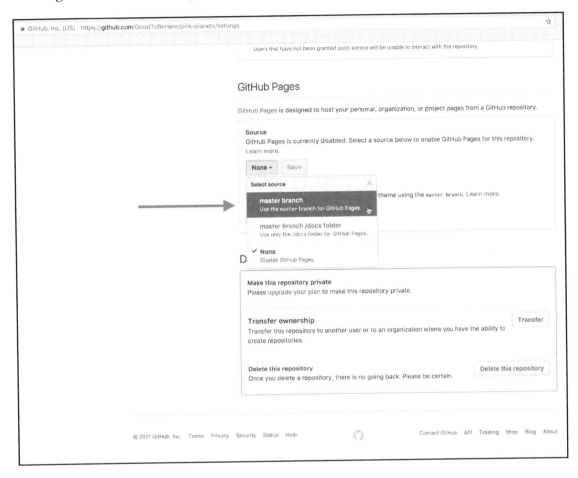

You are nearly there

3. Choose the **master branch** to publish from (we didn't create any other branches, so this is the one) and 4. click on **Save**.

Next, you will see the following message offering you a link to your online project:

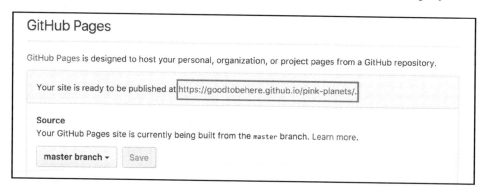

Just one more click!

5. Click it! It might take a moment for the project to take its rightful place, so you might want to wait a painful minute, but eventually, it will be published:

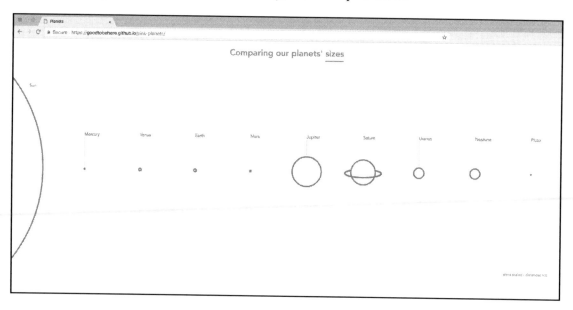

Your published work

Marvelous! Your work is published, and the rest is history! Congratulations.

Our URL is `https://goodtobehere.github.io/pink-planets/`, or more generally, `https://<your username>.github.io/<the repository's name>`. Although this is a logical construct, it might appear a little clunky. You can change it to a custom URL, like we did in our example:

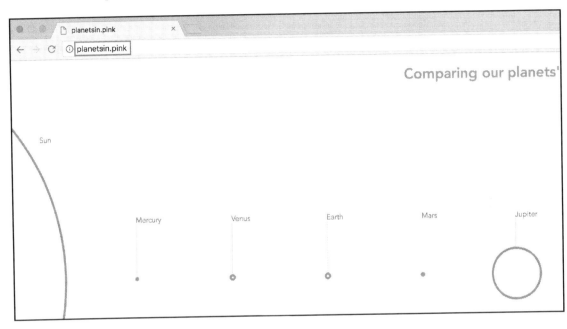

A custom domain

It will require you to use a domain you have secured with the DNS Provider of your choice, and change a few settings on the DNS Provider side as well as, in some cases, on GitHub, but it's also a simple process that you might want to consider.

For excellent guidance regarding a custom domain, check out `https://help.github.com/articles/using-a-custom-domain-with-github-pages/`.

Summary

In this chapter, you learned how to publish your visualization, or in fact any project, on GitHub Pages. You learned what type of pages you can and can't publish on GitHub Pages. You glimpsed the powers of Git and the merits of GitHub before using it as a home for your code. After minor tweaking and prepping, you eventually published your project online. One way to look at this feat is that your project now claims the same online real estate as any other page on the web, which is something to build upon.

Index

Made in the USA
San Bernardino, CA
02 April 2018